do it NOW *do it* FAST *do it* RIGHT™

Storage
Solutions

do it **NOW** *do it* **FAST** *do it* **RIGHT**™

Storage
Solutions

The Taunton Press

Text © 2004 by The Taunton Press, Inc.

Photographs © 2004 by Randy O'Rourke, except © Jason McConathy, p. 28 (top); Schulte Distinctive Storage, www.schulte-storage.com, 1-800-669-3225, pp. 28 (bottom), 29 (top left and right), 31 (top); The Container Store, pp. 29 (bottom), 30 (left), 68 (right and bottom left), 69 (bottom), 84; courtesy of ClosetMaid, pp. 30 (top right), 69 (top); Wall Control photos by Michael Aldredge, pp. 30 (bottom right), 85 (top left); Coleman Storage Images, pp. 31 (bottom), 86 (top right); Roe Osborn, © The Taunton Press, Inc., p. 43 (right); EasyClosets.com, pp. 68 (top left), 85 (right); freedomRail™ by Schulte Distinctive Storage, www.schultestorage.com, 1-800-669-3225, pp. 70 (left and bottom), 71 (right), 86 (bottom right); Schulte Graphics Library, pp. 70–71 (top and bottom), 85 (bottom); © Grey Crawford, p. 86 (left); © Rob Karosis, p. 87; © Knape & Vogt Mfg. Archives, pp. 96 (right), 98, 99; courtesy of Kraft Maid Cabinetry, www.kraftmaid.com, p. 97 (top right and bottom); © Jessie Walker, p. 108 (right); © Sloan Howard, p. 120 (left).

Illustrations © 2004 by The Taunton Press, Inc.

The Taunton Press
Inspiration for hands-on living®

The Taunton Press, Inc., 63 South Main Street, PO Box 5506, Newtown, CT 06470-5506

e-mail: tp@taunton.com

Distributed by Publishers Group West

WRITER AND PROJECT MANAGER: Roy Barnhart

SERIES EDITOR: Tim Snyder

SERIES DESIGN: Lori Wendin

LAYOUT: Cathy Cassidy

ILLUSTRATOR: Charles Lockhart

Taunton's Do It Now/Do It Fast/Do It Right™ is a trademark of
The Taunton Press, Inc., registered in the U.S. Patent and Trademark Office.

LIBRARY OF CONGRESS CATALOGING-IN-PUBLICATION DATA

Storage solutions.

    p. cm. -- (Do it now/do it fast/do it right)

 ISBN 1-56158-668-4

 1. Cabinetwork--Amateurs' manuals. 2. Shelving (Furniture)--Amateurs' manuals. 3. Storage in the home--Amateurs' manuals. I. Taunton Press. II. Series.

 TT197.S847 2004

 648'.8--dc22

               2004003609

Printed in the United States of America
10 9 8 7 6 5 4 3 2 1

The following manufacturers/names appearing in *Storage Solutions* are trademarks: Bosch™; DeWalt®; Elmer's®; Grip Rite™; Irwin™; Phillips®; Porter Cable®; PROBOND®; Skil®; Tapcon®.

Acknowledgments

We're grateful to the contractors, design consultants, and experts whose talent and hard work helped make this book possible. Thanks to Sandra & Christian Hartgens, David Lavalle of Brass Ring Renovators, LLC, Jason Renjilian of Renjilian Enterprises, Timothy Schnurr, Jason Zalinger, and Joanna Zeman. Thanks also to HyLoft USA, Las Vegas, Nevada; Zircon, Campbell, California; and StrongStor, Windquest Companies, Holland, Michigan.

Contents

STORAGE PROJECTS

Garage Makeover 16

With a combination of **SHELVES, RACKS & CABINETS,** you can transform a garage from messy to magnificent

Custom Cabinet 32

Buy the doors, **BUILD THE CASE,** add hinges & finish...you're done!

A Column of Cubbyholes 44

Dressed up with **APPLIED MOLDING** details, this slim set of shelves looks good enough to go anywhere

Closet Makeover 58

Put an end to messy, inefficient closets with **MODULAR COMPONENTS** you can customize to suit your needs

4

58

88

100

110

How to Use This Book

I F YOU'RE INTERESTED IN HOME IMPROVEMENTS that add value and convenience while also enabling you to express your own sense of style, you've come to the right place. **Do It Now/Do It Fast/Do It Right** books are created with an attitude that says "Let's get started!" and an ideal mix of home-improvement inspiration and how-to information. Do It Now books don't skip important steps or force you to guess at what needs to be done to take a project from start to finish.

You'll find that this book has a friendly, easy-to-use format. (See the sample pages shown here.) You'll begin each project knowing exactly what tools and gear you'll need, and what materials to buy at your home center or building-supply outlet. You can get started confidently because every step is illustrated and explained. Along the way, you'll discover plenty of expert advice packed into the margins. For ideas on how to personalize your project, check out the design options pages that follow the step-by-step instructions.

WORK TOGETHER

If you like company when you go to the movies or clean up the kitchen, you'll probably feel the same way about tackling home-improvement projects. The work will go faster, and you'll have a partner to share in the adventure. You'll

Get the TOOLS & GEAR you need. You'll also find out what features and details are important.

DO IT RIGHT tells you what it takes to get top-notch results.

LINGO explains words that the pros know.

WHAT TO BUY helps you put together your project shopping list, so you get all the materials you need.

COOL TOOL puts you in touch with tools that make the job easier.

see that some projects really call for another set of hands to steady a ladder or keep the project going smoothly. Read through the project you'd like to tackle, and note where you're most likely to need help.

PLANNING AND PRACTICE PAY OFF

Most of the projects in this book can easily be completed in a weekend. But the job can take longer if you don't pay attention to planning and project-preparation requirements. Check out the conditions in the area where you'll be working in case repairs are required before you can begin your project. In the GET SET chapter (beginning on the next page), you'll find useful information on getting organized and on many of the tools, fasteners, and glue used in storage projects.

Your skill and confidence will improve with every project you complete. But if you're trying a technique for the first time, it's wise to rehearse before you "go live." This means ordering a little extra in the way of supplies and materials, and finding a location where you can practice your technique.

DESIGN OPTIONS Personalize your project with dimensions, finishes, and details that suit your space and your sense of style.

DO IT NOW helps to keep your project on track with timely advice.

WHAT CAN GO WRONG explains how to avoid common mistakes.

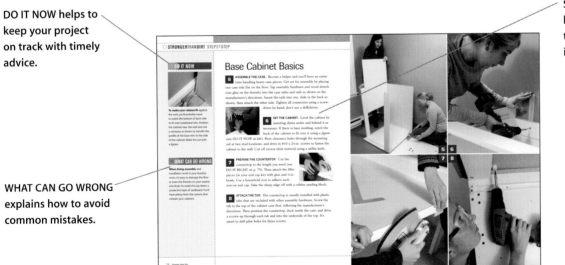

STEP BY STEP Get started, keep going, and finish the job. Every step is illustrated and explained.

Get Set

Rules, Tools to DO IT NOW, DO IT FAST & DO IT RIGHT

ETTING ORGANIZED AND ADDING STORAGE SPACE are goals that go hand in hand. That's why it's important to think about fighting clutter and improving organization when you think about storage. Put the seven steps described on pp. 6–7 to work for you. Then get up to speed on the tools and techniques you'll be using to complete storage projects all over the house. This introductory chapter will help you put effective storage strategies into play and get set to tackle all the projects featured in this book, plus plenty more.

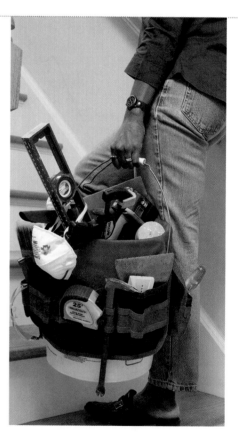

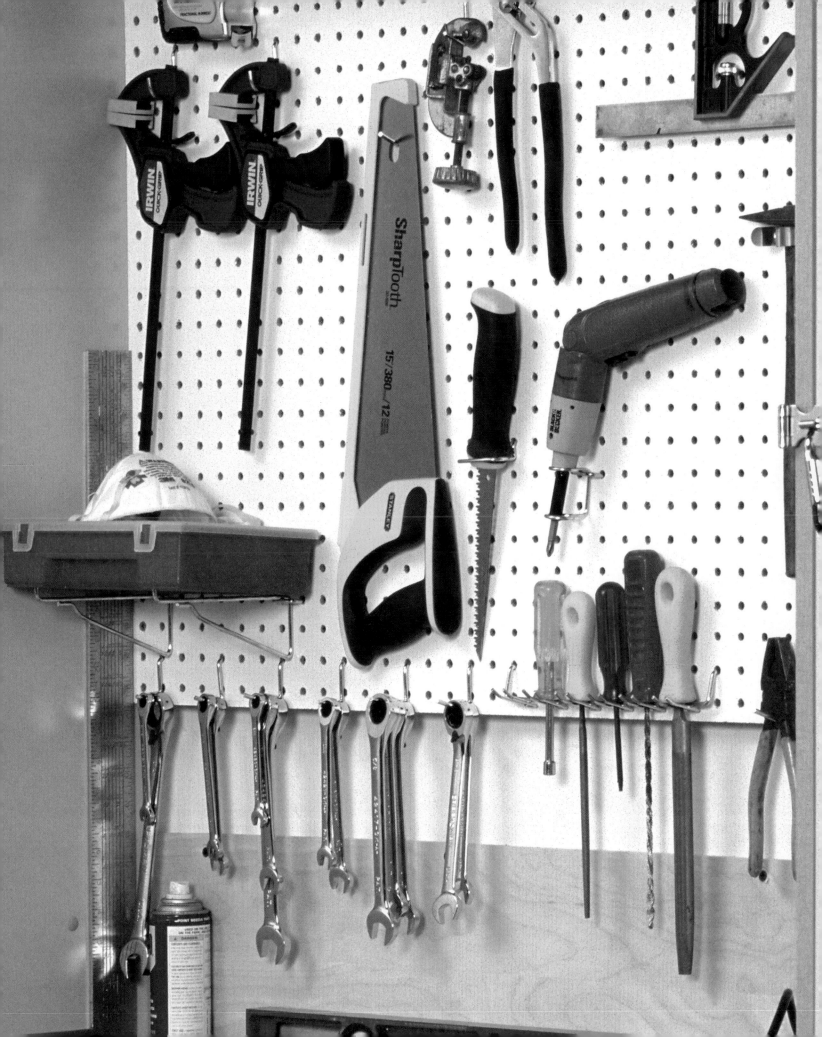

A tag sale (aka garage or yard sale) enables you get paid for getting organized. But it takes a bit of work to pull off a sale successfully. Tag sale tips:

• Give yourself at least a couple of months to collect stuff and get organized.

• Join forces with a neighbor or friend to make your adventure more enjoyable and more profitable.

• Advertise in your local paper and by posting notices on public bulletin boards (in supermarkets and other places).

• Post signs with big, colorful arrows to direct drivers to your house.

• Draw a crowd with refreshments and free stuff. Put this news in your ad.

• Hide or label what's not for sale.

• Expect early birds.

• Plan for rain. Advertise a rain date, or have your sale in a two-car garage.

Let's Get Organized!

Kick off your clutter-conquering campaign with these seven steps.

1. SAVE IT, SELL IT, OR GIVE IT AWAY. Sometimes the best storage solution is to get rid of stuff you don't use. The good news: Thanks to online enterprises like eBay, it's easier than ever to get paid for getting organized. If a cyber garage sale isn't to your liking, try the old-fashioned version. (See the tag sale tips at left.)

2. ASK YOURSELF: HOW OFTEN DO I USE IT? If you haven't used that food processor for months, it doesn't deserve to share countertop space with the toaster you use every day. Don't let low-use stuff make high-use stuff less accessible.

3. FIND THE WASTED SPACE, THEN EXPLOIT IT. Finding "lost" storage space can be just as satisfying as adding new space. For starters, consider the top shelves in kitchen cabinets, the empty space under beds, and unused walls in utility rooms.

4. TACKLE ONE MESS AT A TIME. To promote success as well as sanity, it's important to work on just one room at a time. If you don't have a workshop area, think about getting your garage or basement organized first. (See the projects that begin on p. 16.)

5. HIDE IT, SHOW IT OFF, SWITCH IT AROUND. Storing attractive items on open shelves or on pegs and racks can sometimes free up hidden storage space. Another organizing trick to try is switching things around. For example, moving spare blankets from a closet to the attic will free up closet space.

Flexibility is important. This shelf-and-pole closet system can easily be reconfigured, thanks to the slotted vertical brackets that are mounted on the wall.

Look for durable components. The heavy-gauge coated wire on this sports storage grid and tray is designed to take a beating.

6. BUY, BUILD & IMPROVE. Consider all three options. Ready-made storage solutions (like silverware trays) give you instant organizational improvement. But some things are worth building yourself—not just to save money, but to get the size, style, and features you want. A third option is to improve existing storage.

7. GATHER GREAT IDEAS. We've packed this book with design options, but there are loads of great ideas online and in the aisles of your local home center. Take advantage of these resources as you plan your next storage project.

Hand-Tool Arsenal

Power tools seem to get the best buzzwords: torque, rpm, amps, electronic speed control, and so on. But hand tools are just as important. The tools covered here will give you what it takes to get the dimensions right, mark your cutting and layout lines straight and true, and get essential cutting and joinery work done.

MEASURING & LAYOUT TOOLS

In carpentry language, "layout" can be used as a noun or as a verb. Either way, it refers to the precise work of marking where wood needs to be cut, where fasteners need to be driven, and how parts need to fit.

TAPES, LEVELS, SQUARES & LINES. The most versatile tape to have is a 25-ft. model. A level does more than its name suggests. It also helps you test for vertical or plumb. It's good to have a 2-ft. or 4-ft. level as well as a smaller "torpedo" level. Squares are also important layout tools, and it's good to have three of these: a framing square, a triangle-shaped rafter or Speedsquare, and a combination square.

When you need to mark a long, straight line between two points, a chalkline (aka chalkbox) will get the job done quickly. There's a spool of string and a supply of powdered chalk inside the chalkbox. Stretching

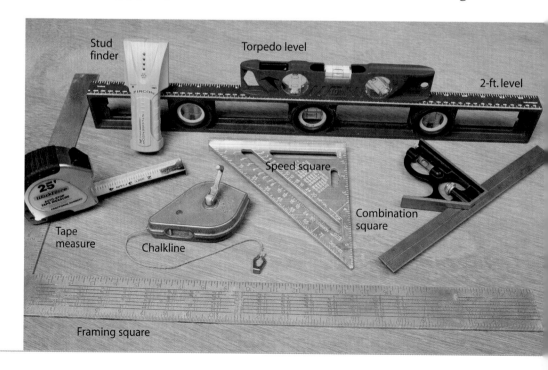

Stud finder

Torpedo level

2-ft. level

Speed square

Tape measure

Chalkline

Combination square

Framing square

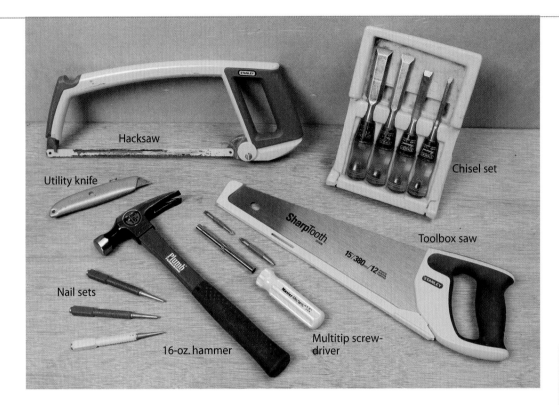

Hacksaw

Utility knife

Chisel set

Nail sets

SharpTooth 15/380mm/12

Toolbox saw

16-oz. hammer

Multitip screw-driver

the line tight and then "snapping" the string leaves a colored layout line.

The only electronic tool in your layout kit is a stud finder. When you move this device along the wall surface, it lights up or beeps when a stud is detected.

CUTTING & FASTENING TOOLS

SAWS & CHISELS. It's smart to have a compact "toolbox" saw handy to handle different cutting jobs. The other saw you need is a hacksaw; it's for cutting metal parts like steel shelving standards. A set of four chisels (¼ in. to 1 in.) will enable you to "chamfer" an angled edge on a sharp corner or to trim a piece of molding to make it fit more precisely. To complete your collection of sharp tools, get a utility knife and a supply of spare blades.

HAMMER, NAIL SETS & A SCREWDRIVER. A 16-oz. hammer is a good size for most interior home-improvement work. Get a hammer that feels comfortable to hold. A nail set is used with your hammer to set nails below the wood surface—something you'll need to do when building a bookcase or cabinet. A $\frac{3}{32}$-in. nail set will handle most of your needs. The last item to acquire for your toolbox is a multitip screwdriver.

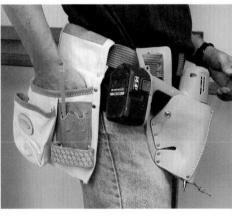

Thanks to a combination of pockets, straps, and holders, a tool belt can improve your efficiency by putting tools and materials within easy reach.

Working safely with power tools goes hand in hand with getting great results. Follow these guidelines:

• Read the owner's manual before you operate the tool.
• Don't wear loose clothing.
• Protect your eyes and ears.
• Always unplug your tool when you are making adjustments, changing blades, or changing bits.
• Use only bits and blades that are sharp and in good condition.
• Make sure that the workpiece is securely supported before you begin cutting, drilling, or sanding.
• Practice on scrap stock first. Making practice cuts will help you make safe, accurate cuts to complete your projects.

Power Up!

Pros know that the right tool will often pay for itself the first time you use it. Good power tools are like that. When used the right way, they not only get the job done quickly, they also deliver the precise results you need for a top-notch job. You can borrow or even rent most of the tools described here. But when you see how much of a difference these tools make in your projects, you'll probably want to own them.

CORDLESS DRILL/DRIVER

A 12-volt or 14-volt model will have plenty of power for most home-improvement projects. Make sure your drill includes an extra battery and a charger. For a bit more money, you can buy cordless tool kits that include a drill, a saw, and even a flashlight. No matter what kind of drill/driver you have, it's important to have some key accessories if you want to get the most from your tool. Essential accessories include a magnetic bit holder; a selection of screw-driving bits; commonly used drill bits for wood, metal, and concrete; and at least one combination countersink/counterbore bit. We like the "drill-and-drive" kits that bundle these items together in a well-designed storage case (see the photo below).

To get the most from any electric drill, buy a "drill-and-drive" kit that includes a quick-change bit holder and a variety of drill and drive bits.

RANDOM-ORBIT SANDER

This power sander can remove wood aggressively or help you create a super-smooth surface in preparation for applying your favorite finish. It all depends on the grit or abrasive rating of the sanding disks that you're using. To keep dust under control, make sure your sander has a dust bag or can be connected to a shop vacuum during use. Stock up on sanding disks in a variety of grits. If you have grits from 80 to 220, you'll be ready for any sanding assignment.

JIGSAW

This compact saw is what you need to make curved cuts. But it's also a good tool for cutting notches and making inside cuts that have to be started by drilling a hole somewhere in the middle of the workpiece. Variable-speed control is a good feature to have on a jigsaw; it gives you more control. If you have a small hand, you'll probably prefer a "top-handle" model to a barrel-grip model. Buy a variety of blades designed to fit your saw, and make sure to practice some curved cuts before you make one for a project.

Jigsaws are for curves and cutouts. Barrel-grip and top-handle models are available. You can also choose between corded and cordless.

CIRCULAR SAW

Construction crews use these saws to make rough cuts in framing lumber and sheathing panels. But your circular saw can also do fine work, such as making bookcases, shelves, and cabinets. The key is to use a finish-cutting blade in your saw and to use tips and techniques we'll demonstrate in this book. There are many circular-saw models available, but price is often an indication of quality in this tool category. Make a trip to your home center and try before you buy. Look for a saw that you can grip comfortably with both hands. Easy-to-use bevel and depth controls are also important.

WHAT CAN GO WRONG

OK, so you drove a nail where you shouldn't have. It's a mistake we all make from time to time. When the nail absolutely has to come out, you can pull it using a cat's paw, a special prybar designed to grab the nail just below its head, and lever it up so you can finish the pull-out with your hammer. Patch over the resulting hole with some wood putty.

Get It Together

Let's face it: Most home-improvement projects involve putting things together. That's why a bit of basic information on fasteners and adhesives can be helpful.

FINISHING NAILS & BRADS

Finishing nails and brads are the nails you need for building bookcases, cabinets, and other interior projects. These nails have smaller heads than common nails because they usually have to be set below the wood surface so the nails can be hidden with wood putty.

PENNIES & GAUGES. Finishing nails are described by their "penny" size, which is shown as 4d, 6d, 8d, etc. A 4d finishing nail measures 1¼ in. long, while an 8d finishing nail is 2 in. long. Brads look like mini-finishing nails; they're described by their length and the gauge (diameter) of the wire used to make them.

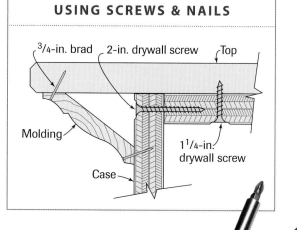

USING SCREWS & NAILS

3/4-in. brad · 2-in. drywall screw · Top · Molding · Case · 1¼-in. drywall screw

DRIVING, SETTING & FILLING. If you're nailing in a location that's going to show in the finished project, leave the head of the nail (or brad) just above the surface of the wood. Then use a hammer and nail set to drive the head of the nail ⅛ in. or so below the wood surface. Nice job. You've just "set" the nail. Now you can fill the hole with a dab of wood putty.

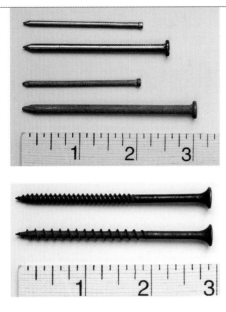

SCREWS

Screws have loads more holding power than nails, and they're easier than ever to use, thanks to all of the quick-change "drill-and-drive" accessories available (see photo on p. 10).

THREADS & HEADS. It's smart to have a selection of "drywall" screws in lengths ranging from ¾ in. to 3 in. This type of screw has a "bugle" head, with a cross-shaped Phillips recess. "Coarse-thread" screws are usually better than "fine-thread" versions when you're joining wood parts together. Black-colored drywall screws are what to use for interior projects.

PILOT HOLES. In most cases, you'll need to drill a pilot hole before driving a screw. The hole should be about the same diameter as the diameter of the screw, excluding its threads. The best way to drill pilot holes for screws is with a combination countersink/counterbore bit (see photo at right).

GLUE, CAULK & PUTTY

It's amazing how many ways there are to stick things together. But for most storage projects, just a few types of goo will do. Here they are:

YELLOW WOOD GLUE. This is the best adhesive to use for interior wood-to-wood joints. Hold glued parts together with clamps, or by driving screws or nails, until the glue dries, or "sets," in about 45 minutes.

LATEX CAULK. This water-based caulk (aka acrylic caulk or sealant) does a good job of filling gaps (between the back of a cabinet and the wall, for example).

WOOD PUTTY. Use this dough-like filler to fill nail holes, to cover countersunk screws, and to fill any other holes or depressions that shouldn't be in the wood surface. Always overfill the hole, then sand your patch smooth after the putty has dried.

When drilling large-diameter holes in particularly hard concrete, start with a $\frac{1}{8}$-in.-dia. bit and incrementally increase drill-bit sizes. It's easier on you, the bits, and the tool!

Fastening Things to the Wall

Whether you're tackling a closet makeover (p. 58), installing coated wire shelves (p. 82), or adding a medicine cabinet in the bathroom (p. 32), storage projects often require fastening things to the wall. Your fastening strategy depends on the type of wall you're working with and on the amount of weight you need to support.

FASTENING INTO STUDS

Here's a rule you can count on: Always fasten into a stud if possible. Studs and other "2x" framing members provide solid backing for nails and screws.

STUD-FINDING STRATEGIES. An electronic stud finder is designed to detect studs accurately enough so that you can even mark the 1½-in. thickness of the stud on the wall. A stud finder will also identify other framing members hidden in the wall. Keep in mind that studs are spaced on 16-in. or 24-in. centers.

SCREWS VS. NAILS. If you're fastening into a stud, it's better to drive a screw than a nail. Screws have more holding power, and it's easier to remove them without damaging the wall or anything else. At least half of a screw's total length should extend into the stud.

HOLLOW-WALL & MASONRY FASTENERS

There are plenty of times when it's not possible to fasten into studs. That's where hollow-wall fasteners and masonry anchors come in. There are quite a few of these fasteners available, but it's not that difficult to select the anchor that's right for your particular job.

Most hollow-wall anchors are designed for use in gypsum board or drywall. Check the package label to make sure the anchor is suitable for the load, the type of wall, and the wall thickness.

TOGGLES & MOLLIES. Hollow-wall fasteners have a variety of other names. But you'll find these gizmos in the same aisle where screws are stocked. Go to your home center or hardware store armed with some key information: the kind of wall you are working on (drywall, plaster, or paneling); wall thickness; and the amount of weight you need to support. Read the manufacturer's information on the packaging material to find the best hollow-wall fastener for your application.

MASONRY ANCHORS. When you need to fasten into concrete or brick, the first step is to bore a hole using a masonry bit. Then you can wedge a hollow plastic plug into the hole and drive a screw into the center of the plug. This fastening technique is fine for light-to-medium loads (up to 25 lb. or so). Plan B is to buy some self-tapping masonry screws (Tapcon® is a common brand) and a matching bit for installing them. The hole you bore is sized so that the special screw will cut its own threads in the masonry as you drive it (see photo below). Once you get the hang of using this system, you'll find it quick, easy, and strong. For best results, buy your self-tapping screws with hex heads, and use a matching driver in your cordless drill to drive the fasteners.

Sleeve-type anchors like these are designed to be used in masonry walls. Driving a screw wedges the anchor tight in its hole.

The fastest way to anchor into concrete is by driving a special self-tapping screw into a predrilled hole. A hex-head screw is easy to drive with a matching bit chucked in your drill.

Garage Makeover

With a combination of **SHELVES, RACKS & CABINETS**, you can transform a garage from messy to magnificent

SOONER OR LATER, you have to deal with the jumble of odd but essential stuff that fills your garage. This makeover plan is sure to help out in three major ways. First, we'll install a sturdy cabinet, countertop, and pegboard combination that gives you storage space and a compact workshop setup. Second on the list is a heavy-duty shelf that will (finally!) get bulky items out of your way. The final clutter-control weapon is a storage rack made from 1x4 pine boards. This wooden grid is a great place to hang garden tools, extension cords, ladders, and anything else that you haven't already stowed. Let's dig in; the best-organized garage in your neighborhood begins here.

| INSTALL CABINETS | INSTALL HIGH SHELVES | FIGURE OUT THE LAYOUT | INSTALL A TOOL RACK |

+ WHAT CAN GO WRONG

It can be difficult to judge distance when parking your car in tight quarters. To make sure you don't hit your new cabinets when pulling your car into the garage, hang an old tennis ball from a string that contacts the windshield at the point you want to stop.

✳ WHAT'S DIFFERENT?

"Drywall" screws are available with fine and coarse threads. The fine ones work best on metal studs. Use coarse-thread screws in wood.

Tools & Gear

With a couple of exceptions in each case, the tools required for all three projects are the same.

FOR ALL PROJECTS...

LEVELS. To keep your installations level and plumb, you'll need a 2-ft. level and a torpedo level.

STUD FINDER. You need to find the studs before you put up your shelves and tool rack.

TAPE MEASURE. For this job, a 25-ft. tape will serve you best.

CORDLESS DRILL/DRIVER. To avoid unnecessary delays, make sure that you've got two fully charged batteries before you begin.

DRILL ACCESSORIES. A quick-change "drill-and-drive" kit will help you to work faster. Your kit should include a #2 Phillips bit, a selection of small-diameter drill bits ($\frac{1}{16}$ in. to $\frac{1}{4}$ in.), a $\frac{7}{16}$-in. hex-head diver, and a #6 combination countersink/counterbore bit.

STEP LADDER. A 4-ft. to 6-ft. ladder will help you with installation work that needs to happen at overhead heights.

RUBBER MALLET. Since it delivers a cushioned blow, this mallet is helpful when assembling cabinets. If you don't have one, it's OK to cushion the blow from a regular hammer with a block of wood.

BAR CLAMPS. Thirty-in.-long ones will work for clamping the trays during assembly.

SAW. You'll need a circular saw or a crosscut handsaw to build the storage rack.

RAFTER SQUARE. This triangular "speedsquare" also does a good job of guiding your circular saw when cutting boards to length.

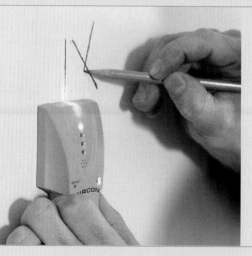

COOL TOOL

Electronic sensors (aka stud finders) do a quick and foolproof job of finding studs, ceiling joists, and other framing members. Simple models flash or beep when the device is over the center of a stud. This model shines a light line at the edge of the stud. More expensive versions can even detect hidden wiring and plumbing pipes.

What to Buy

Since there are three different storage projects featured in this chapter, your shopping list depends on which project(s) you're doing. That's why the list is divided below.

CABINET/WORKBENCH/PEGBOARD COMBINATION

Different cabinet combinations are available to fit your budget and the space available in your garage. If you can't find garage-style cabinets like those discussed here, you can use ready-to-assemble cabinets like those featured in our laundry room makeover (p. 72). Either way, cabinets include all assembly hardware.

HEAVY-DUTY SHELF

The shelf system discussed here comes in kit form, with a pair of 48-in.-long shelves, four support brackets, and mounting screws. Other heavy-duty shelving options are also available, including steel brackets that can support wood shelves that you purchase and cut separately.

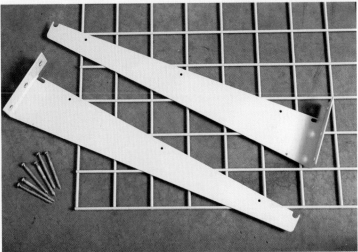

GARDEN TOOL RACK

To build and install a 12-ft. rack like the one discussed here, use the following shopping list:

LUMBER.   Get 14 ft. of 1x2 pine or spruce for the vertical battens. For the horizontal boards, you'll need five 12-ft. 1x4s.

FASTENERS.   Buy a 1-lb. box of 2 1/2-in. deck screws.

HOOKS & HANGERS.   You can have some fun here. Make a list of all the tools and items you'd like to hang on your rack, and note what kind of hardware you need to support this gear. Make sure to get installation screws as necessary, so you can mount your hangers on the rack.

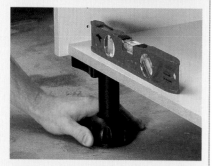
Assembling Cabinets

1 **ASSEMBLE THE CABINETS.** The cabinet parts and the assembly hardware will come in the box. Attach the top, bottom, and (on tall cabinets) fixed center shelf to the side panels. Then attach the cleats, inserting screws into factory-drilled holes. Fasten the mounting plates for the legs to the bottom front edge of the cabinet, then screw the legs in all the way.

2 **ASSEMBLE THE DRAWERS.** For units with drawers, assemble each drawer case by fitting all four case sides around the drawer bottom. Secure corner joints with glued wooden dowels inserted in predrilled holes. Attach the handle to the drawer front, then loosely attach the front to the drawer case with screws.

3 **INSTALL THE DRAWER SLIDES.** Attach a drawer slide to the bottom edge of a drawer, flush with the front edge. Secure the mating slide to the side of the cabinet. This should be quick and easy, since holes for installation screws have been predrilled at the factory. Repeat this step for all drawer-slide hardware.

4 **POSITION & LEVEL THE CABINETS.** The smartest strategy here is to position and level the tallest cabinet first, then level the others to it. When the cabinet is roughly in position, mark stud locations on the wall, just below the bottom edge of the installation cleat. Position the cabinets against the wall and screw the legs up or down to get the cabinets level and plumb.

:: DO IT FAST

The fastest way to install cabinets against a concrete or concrete-block wall is to use 2-in. Tapcon screws. Bore a ¼-in.-dia. clearance hole through the cleat on the back of the cabinet. Then use the special masonry bit that comes with your Tapcon screws to bore installation holes in the concrete. You can drive these screws using a nut driver or a socket wrench, as shown here.

⊙ DO IT RIGHT

To align the drawer front with the benchtop and cabinet sides, close the drawer, make adjustments, and, while holding the pieces together, slide the drawer open while a helper applies clamps. Tighten the screws. Check the alignment, and drive two 1-in. screws through the drawer case and into the false front.

Installing Everything

5 **INSTALL THE FLOOR CABINETS.** Use a ³⁄₁₆-in.-dia. bit to drill two installation holes in the top cleat and two in the bottom cleat. To fasten the bottom cleat against a concrete wall, drive Tapcon screws as we did here, or use a heavy-duty masonry anchor. Use heavy-duty drywall anchors to fasten the top cleat against drywall. Insert wood shims behind cleats if necessary to keep cabinets plumb.

6 **INSTALL THE BENCHTOP.** Place the benchtop on the base cabinet and rest any unsupported end on a clamp. Using a #6 combination bit, bore three countersunk pilot holes through the cabinet side and into the edge of the top. Then drive in 2-in. screws. Similarly, connect the adjoining cabinets, but with 1¼-in. screws.

7 **INSTALL WALL CABINETS.** The wall cabinets used here are designed to be supported by a rail screwed to the wall. Install the rail following the manufacturer's instructions, making sure to keep it level and at the proper height. Hang the cabinet on the rail, and drive extra installation screws through the top and bottom rails and into studs or drywall anchors, as in step 5.

8 **INSTALL DOORS.** Attach the hinges to the door and the mounting plates to the cabinet with screws. Engage the hinges on the mounting plates and tighten the mounting screws. Make side, height, and depth adjustments to fit the door squarely over its opening. Nice work so far; your cabinet-workbench combination is looking good.

5

6

7

8

Installing Heavy-Duty Shelves

Chuck a ⁷⁄₁₆-in. hex driver in your drill/driver for speedy installation of the 4-in. lag screws. If your cordless drill/driver is overpowered by this task, you may need to use a corded drill. It also helps to spray the lags with silicone lubricant before driving.

Large plastic tubs are great for storing smaller items and anything that needs protection from dust and moisture. Look for clear plastic boxes if you need to see what's inside. Or simply stick on a label.

9 **LOCATE THE SHELF.** With this type of shelving, your best bet is to set shelf height high on the wall, but within reach. Mark a level line on the wall at the planned height of your shelf. You can use a regular level or a laser model. Extend the line about 2 ft. longer than the planned length of the shelf being installed.

10 **MARK STUD LOCATIONS.** Using a stud finder, locate your first stud. Then measure 16 in. from the stud's approximate center and test for a neighboring stud. Keep marking stud locations along your shelf line.

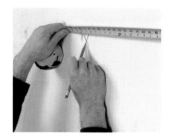

11 **INSTALL SHELF BRACKETS.** Hold each shelf bracket in place on the line and centered over a stud location. Trace the bracket's mounting holes onto the wall in pencil. Remove the bracket to drill pilot holes for installation screws. Reposition the bracket and secure it with the lag screws that come in the kit (see also DO IT FAST at left).

12 **INSTALL SHELF SECTIONS.** Place shelves atop the brackets following the manufacturer's instructions. Secure each shelf section to holes in the brackets and to neighboring shelf sections with plastic tie-straps. That's it. Now you can load 'em up.

9 10
11 12

It's a lot easier to determine accessory placement if you make a temporary version of the rack on the floor, perhaps tacking on two or three battens. Then position the tools, etc. and pre-install the accessories. Tip: Make a quick sketch or take a digital photo so you remember what goes where later!

Rack 'Em Up!

13 **CUT & SAND THE PARTS.** Cut your long 1x4s to a uniform final length using a circular saw or cutting by hand with a cross-cut saw. Using sandpaper wrapped around a sanding block, smooth rough edges and round over sharp corners. Stain or varnish the boards for a more finished appearance, if you wish. Hey, with a garage, every little bit helps!

14 **HOOK UP!** Space your boards evenly apart on the garage floor, just as they'll be installed on the wall. You can temporarily tack a couple of battens across the boards to hold them in place, if necessary. Next, position the tools and other stuff you want to store on the rack. Select and install the best hooks and other hang-up hardware, drilling pilot holes and driving screws as necessary.

15 **INSTALL THE BATTENS.** Mark stud locations on the wall, and establish a level line to determine where the top or bottom of each batten will be. Locate the studs just as you did in step 10. Then use your drill/driver to screw battens to the wall at these locations. Install each batten with three 2½-in. deck screws.

16 **ATTACH THE BOARDS.** Use your drill/driver to screw each board in place across the battens. Keep a uniform space (we used 1 in.) between boards, and use a pair of screws at each batten connection. To avoid splitting the batten, it's best to drill pilot holes for your screws. When your last board is in place, load up your rack and listen carefully: Your car is saying "thanks."

Slat wall systems are based on slotted wall panels designed to hold a variety of specially made hangers and storage fixtures.

Versatility is usually important when you're shopping for a sport storage rack.

The key to organizing a garage is to move stuff from the floor to the walls by making use of every vertical inch of space. The challenge is to find the right combination of hooks, hangers, and specialized hardware for all your gear. Keep tools and toys accessible, but do the opposite for solvents and other dangerous materials. Once you get your garage organized, it's much easier to keep it that way.

Individual hooks and a wire grid system combine to get this garage wall organized.

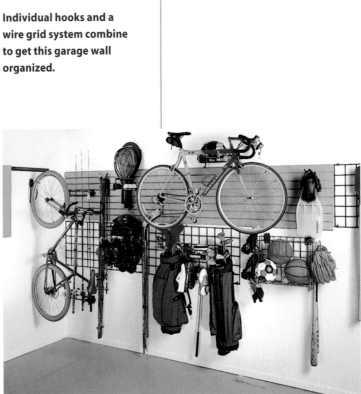

Bikes used to be awkward to store for easy retrieval, but two workable ways are shown here.

A heavy-duty standard-and-bracket system gives you shelf space that's adjustable. A folding step stool provides easy access to high shelves.

These heavy-duty adjustable shelves are easy to install, thanks to a horizontal mounting track that you screw to the wall as a support for the vertical standards.

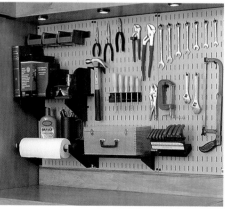

A combination of shelves and cabinets is often the best storage strategy in garage and utility-room areas.

Pegboard paved the way for this slotted wall panel designed to hold different hooks, hangers, and shelf supports

Closed storage is ideal for chemicals, paints, and other items that should stay clear of kids. A garage can get pretty dirty, too, so doors cut down on dust.

Not all cabinets are meant for the kitchen. This rugged cabinet system is designed to provide storage and work-shop space—a great storage solution in a garage, basement, shed, or utility room.

Custom Cabinet

Buy the doors, BUILD THE CASE, add hinges & finish…you're done!

I F YOU NEED MORE STORAGE SPACE in your bathroom (and who doesn't?), this shallow cabinet is a great solution. You don't have to be a cabinet-maker to build a great-looking cabinet. Here's the secret: Skip the trickiest part of the construction process by ordering a pair of doors in the style and size you want. Build the case, hinge the doors, add the shelves, and then complete your cabinet with hardware and finish. See, it's not that difficult. Your homemade cabinet will cost a fraction of what you'd pay for a factory-made version, and you get the freedom to build yours exactly the right size. Let's get started!

BUILD THE CASE   ADD TRIM   INSTALL HARDWARE   HANG THE CABINET

Tools & Gear

Getting doors to align perfectly is tricky. If there's an uneven gap between doors after they're installed, don't worry. You can realign them. Note which hinges need to be shifted slightly, then remove them. Plug the old holes with a wood match dipped in glue, then drill new mounting holes and reposition the hinge. If your doors hit each other when closing, you can use a block plane to plane a bevel on the center edges.

MITER BOX. You'll need a good miter box or chopsaw to make miter and square cuts.

CIRCULAR SAW. To make smooth, accurate cuts in the plywood parts, put a sharp finish-cutting blade in your circular saw and get a straightedge to guide the saw as you cut.

CLOTHES IRON. Huh? That's right! You'll need one to apply the iron-on wood edging.

SQUARES. A combination square and a framing square will both be useful.

CLAMPS. A couple of long bar clamps and several spring clamps will make it easier for you to assemble the cabinet, especially if you're working alone.

CORDLESS DRILL/DRIVER. This tool will get a workout on this project, so make sure your batteries are charged. Have a drill index handy, as well as driver bits for Phillips-head and trim-head screws. You'll also find it helpful to have a small Vix bit to use when mounting hinges.

RANDOM-ORBIT SANDER. A power sander will speed the smoothing work you need to do prior to applying finish. If you don't have a random-orbit sander, a small oscillating pad sander will do.

A *rip* is a sawcut made parallel to the grain direction, generally along the length of a board or panel. A *crosscut* describes a cut made perpendicular to the grain, generally across a board or panel. When cutting parts for a cabinet, you usually rip to width first, then cut to length.

What to Buy

1 CABINET DOORS. Order doors at your home center or from a cabinet dealer. You'll be able to select the size, the wood species, the finish, and the style of panel that's held in the frame. Delivery typically takes two to four weeks.

2 ³/₄-IN. PLYWOOD. Buy enough birch plywood to make the case, top, and shelves. We used a 4x4 sheet for this cabinet.

3 1X2 PINE OR POPLAR. A 6-ft. length will do.

4 BEADBOARD PANELING. Get a half sheet of this ¹/₄-in.-thick plywood paneling to use for the back of the cabinet.

5 BED MOLDING. This molding is part of the cornice design. Buy a 6-ft. length.

6 ³/₄-IN. SCREEN MOLDING. This small molding is ¹/₄ in. thick and ³/₄ in. wide. You'll need about 6 ft.

7 BIRCH EDGEBANDING. This iron-on wood edging covers plywood edges. One roll will do.

8 FASTENERS. You'll need one box each of ³/₄-in. brads, 3d finishing nails, 1¹/₄-in. drywall screws, and 1⁵/₈-in. trim-head screws.

9 HINGES. We used four "no-mortise" hinges on this cabinet because they eliminate the need to chisel out mortises. If you can't find these hinges at your local home center, a woodworking or cabinet-hardware catalog will have them.

10 HANDLE & CATCH. Buy a dual magnetic catch—one designed for a pair of doors. You'll also need to choose handles for your doors.

11 SHELF SUPPORTS. The supports we used in this cabinet are designed to fit in ¹/₄-in.-dia. holes. You'll find these shelf support pins in different finishes and styles.

12 SANDPAPER. Buy several sheets of 120-grit sandpaper for smoothing the wood prior to painting.

13 WOOD PUTTY. You'll need some to fill nail holes.

14 WOOD GLUE. Yellow wood glue is best for this project.

15 PRIMER & PAINT. Get a quick-drying primer and some acrylic semigloss trim paint.

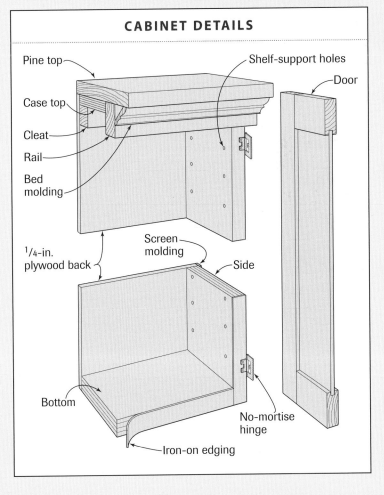

CABINET DETAILS

Pine top
Case top
Cleat
Rail
Bed molding
Shelf-support holes
Door
¹/₄-in. plywood back
Screen molding
Side
Bottom
No-mortise hinge
Iron-on edging

Building the Case

1 **CUT THE CASE PARTS.** We're talking about the case sides, bottom, top, back, and all the shelves you plan to use (see the drawing on p. 35). With your plywood supported by 2x4s, make rip cuts first, guiding your circular saw against a straightedge that's clamped to the plywood. Then cut your case parts to their finished lengths.

2 **MAKE HOLES FOR SHELF SUPPORTS.** To get this boring work done quickly and accurately, use a pegboard jig to guide your ¼-in.-dia. drill bit. A cleat screwed to the pegboard registers the jig against the edge of each side. Wrap tape around the drill bit so that the depth of each hole is ½ in.

3 **ASSEMBLE THE CASE.** Screw two cleats to your worktable so that they form a right angle. Use this setup to help you position the case sides, top, and bottom when assembling the case. Bore pilot holes for a pair of 1⅝-in. trim-head screws at each joint, then spread glue  on mating parts, brace the joint tight, and drive the screws. An extra set of hands is helpful here, but you can also use clamps to hold case parts against the cleats.

4 **ATTACH THE BACK.** Make sure the case is square (see WHAT CAN GO WRONG at left). Then spread some glue on the back edges of the case, and attach the back with ¾-in. brads. You can space the brads about 10 in. apart. When you've finished nailing the back, wipe off glue squeeze-out with a damp cloth. Turn the case over on its back, and wipe excess glue from the interior, too.

1

2

3

4

The molding needs to be placed upside-down in your miter box. Pretend the vertical fence of the miter box is the side of the cabinet. Clamp a block of wood to the miter box bed that will hold the molding securely.

Melted glue from iron-on edging can gum up the surface of your clothes iron. To keep peace in the family, protect the working surface of the iron with a layer of aluminum foil when applying your wood edging.

Adding Trim & Moldings

5 **ATTACH THE CLEAT, RAIL & TOP.** As shown in the drawing on p. 35, this case has a top rail and a cleat. Install these two parts with glue and trim-head screws, making sure to drill pilot holes for screws first. You can drive three or four screws down through the case top and into the cleat. Screw the rail to the front edge of the case top. Then attach the pine (or poplar) top by driving 1¼-in. drywall screws through the underside of the case top.

6 **ADD THE CORNICE.** Hold a length of molding in position on one side of the cabinet, mark where the miter cut needs to be, then cut it on your miter saw (see DO IT RIGHT at left). Drill pilot holes and drive nails only partway in to "tack" this piece in place. Mark, cut, and tack the long front piece and the remaining side piece. When you're satisfied with the fit, glue and nail the cornice in place. Spring clamps provide extra holding power until the glue sets.

7 **TRIM THE SIDES.** To conceal the edges of the plywood back along the sides of the cabinet, cover this joint with ¾-in. screen molding. Cut the two pieces of molding to fit, then use your finger or a small brush to spread glue on the back of each piece. Fasten the molding to the case sides with ¾-in. brads.

8 **IRON ON SOME EDGING.** Cut three pieces of wood edging to rough lengths (an inch or so longer than necessary) for the side and bottom edges of the case. Use a utility knife to make square end cuts. Hold each piece of edging on its case edge and iron it in place. Edge the sides first, allowing the excess edging to extend beyond the bottom of the case. Trim this excess with your utility knife, then cut the bottom edging piece to fit between the side pieces and iron it on.

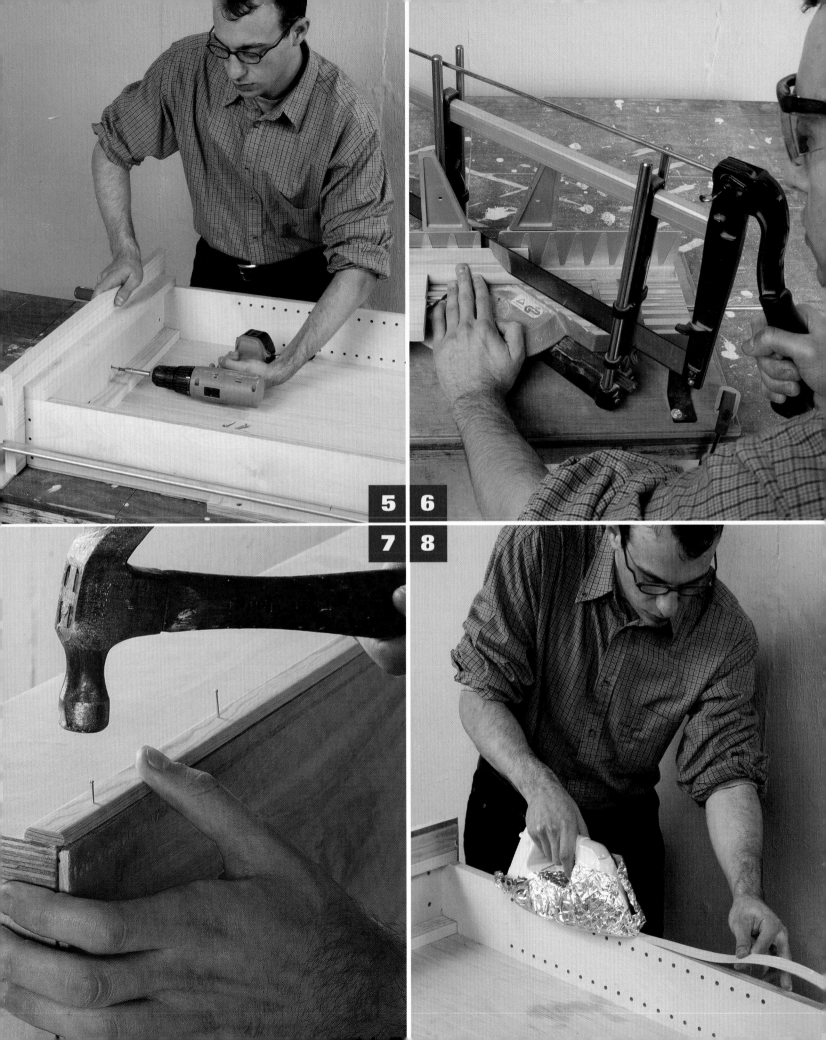

5

6

7

8

To avoid wasted steps, start by installing each hinge with only one or two screws, then test the fit of your doors. If you need to reposition the hinges slightly, it won't be necessary to fill and redrill so many screw holes.

✳ WHAT'S DIFFERENT?

Trim-head screws are designed to be used like finishing nails, but they've got the holding power of screws, so they're great for assembling cabinet cases. A trim-head screw has a smaller head than a regular screw, and there's a square recess in the head where a matching bit fits.

Final Touches & Installation

9 **INSTALL THE HINGES.** Mark the hinge locations on the case sides, then hold the hinges in position while drilling pilot holes with a Vix bit. When all hinges are screwed to the case, get a helper or some wood supports to hold each door open while you drill pilot holes and drive remaining screws. Check to make sure the doors are aligned and operate freely. Then detach the doors and hinges in preparation for finishing the cabinet.

10 **FINISH IT.** Fill all holes and gaps with wood putty, then give the case and doors a thorough sanding with 150-grit sandpaper. Ease sharp edges and smooth out surface irregularities. Get the dust off by vacuuming and wiping with a damp cloth. Now you're ready for primer and paint. Apply one coat of fast-drying primer and two coats of semigloss paint.

11 **INSTALL KNOBS & CATCHES.** Measure, mark, and drill holes for the knobs or handles you've bought, then install them. Depending on the type of magnetic catch you have, it may be necessary to glue and screw a mounting block to the top rail in order to install the catch. Attach a mating metal plate on the back of each door.

12 **HANG IT, THEN FILL IT.** Your installation screws should be driven through the cleat, through the wallboard, and into studs or heavy-duty drywall anchors. Locate two studs behind the planned cabinet location, then have a helper hold the cabinet in position while you transfer stud marks to the cabinet. Drill ⅛-in.-dia. pilot holes through the cleat for 2½-in.-long mounting screws. Keep the cabinet level as you drive the screws. Now you can remount the doors and install shelves.

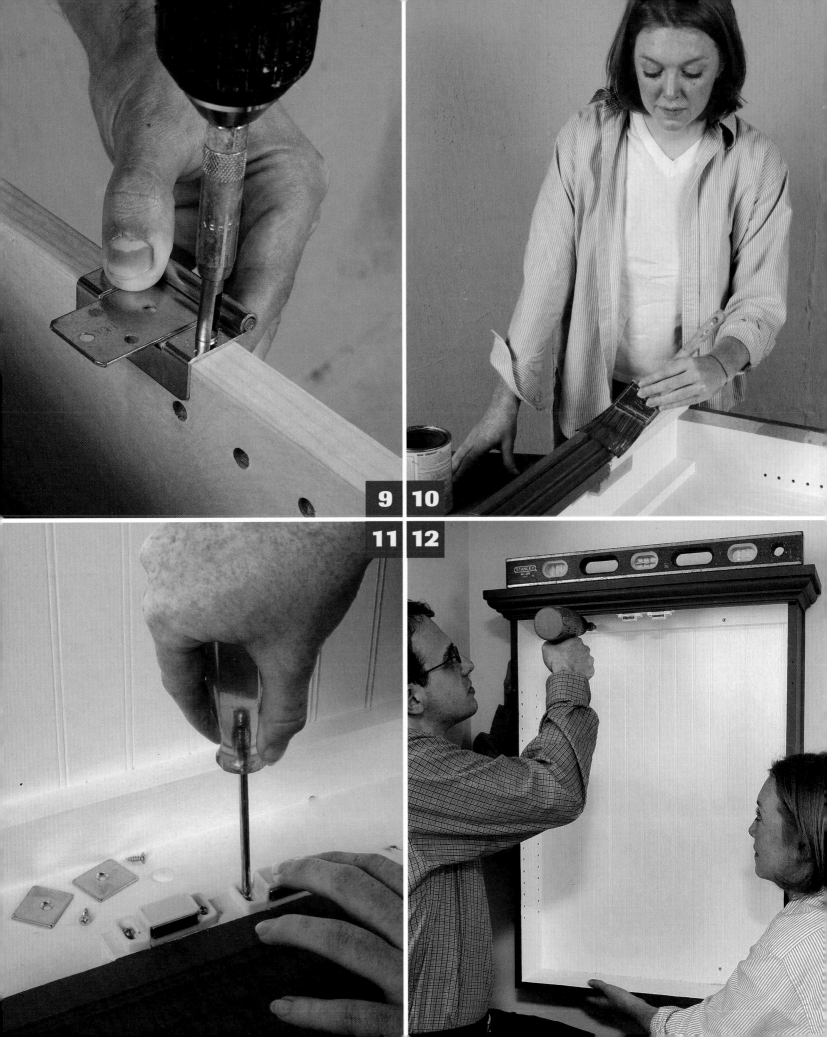

9 10

11 12

A medicine cabinet usually needs to be shallow. But by building out the top with molding and a wider board, you create ample display space.

Fill your own prescription for a bathroom cabinet by

choosing premade doors and shelf systems, along with hardware. Your only constraints are door size and shelf depth. There's no shortage of choice when it comes to style or color, or you can paint or stain premade doors yourself. Since you're the boss, you can beef up trim to make a custom-cabinet look. After all, it is mostly custom-built—by you.

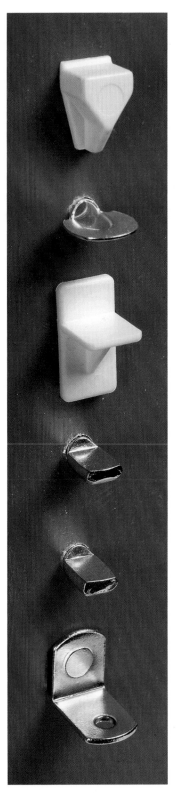

Doors are tough to make but easy to order premade, and there are many styles, colors, and sizes available. Look for a finish that stands up to humidity and is easy to clean.

If you want to do more than build a basic case, you'll find many variations possible. This oak cabinet has custom doors and a marble shelf.

Shelf supports are available in different styles and finishes. You'll need four supports for each shelf.

43

A Column of Cubbyholes

Dressed up with **APPLIED MOLDING** details, this slim set of shelves looks good enough to go anywhere

ERE'S A PROJECT THAT CAN BE HAPPY and helpful wherever a slim measure of shelf space is needed. This storage column has a pine top that sits on a crown of mitered molding. The sides have a frame-and-panel appearance, while the front edges are finished off with beaded trim. Most of these details are borrowed from classic bookcase construction, but the slimmed-down size means you can put these shelves in many different locations. You may want to build several units instead of just one. Or you can try one of the design variations shown on pp. 56–57.

BUILD THE CASE   ADD TRIM   MITER THE MOLDING   SAND & FINISH

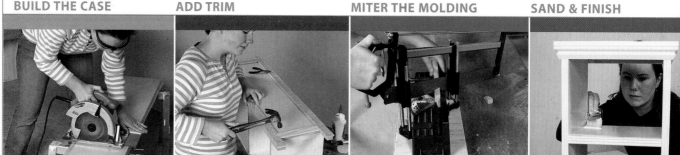

▶ DO IT RIGHT

Before putting your circular saw to work, check to make sure the blade is square to the base. You'll need a small square to do this. If necessary, loosen the saw's bevel-cutting adjustment and reset the cutting angle to exactly 90 degrees.

■ LINGO

Many cabinets and cases (including this one) are built in frame-and-panel style. The frame members along the outside edges are either vertical *stiles* or horizontal *rails*. The panel fills the center.

Tools & Gear

Keep your basic tool kit handy because you'll need a hammer, tape measure, and framing square for this project. You'll also need this extra gear:

CIRCULAR SAW. Just the tool for cutting the plywood and paneling to size. To get perfectly straight cuts, check out the guide shown on p. 49.

FINISH-CUTTING BLADE. This carbide-tipped blade has 40 teeth and is designed to make super-smooth "finish" cuts in solid wood as well as in plywood and other composite-wood panels. The 7-7 1/4-in. size fits most circular saws. Different brands are available.

DRILL. You'll need one to predrill holes for nails and screws.

MITER BOX. To make exact cuts in molding and other small pieces of wood, you'll need a miter box that comes with its own fine-tooth saw. The box is designed to hold the wood and guide the sawblade for cuts at different angles. A good hand miter box like the one shown here will cost around $40. Less-expensive versions are also available.

Art. No. TK
freu
7-7 1/4" Fir
PREMIUM QUALITY C
40 TEETH
THIN KERF
ADVANCED ANTI-KIC

Rip Wood
Crosscut Wood
Chip Board
Plywood
Non-Ferrous   Not Recommended
Melamine

Fair   G
Copyright of Freu

ALWAYS WEAR SAFE
AND USE SAFET

COOL TOOL

Nothing beats a jigsaw when it comes to cutting curves. But a jigsaw also excels at making square-edged cutouts, as you need to do when cutting the legs out of the sides (step 5). The best type of jigsaw to buy is one with variable-speed control, so you can adjust the cutting speed (strokes per minute) to match the material. Also look for orbital action, a feature that helps the saw cut faster.

What to Buy

LUMBER ORDER

1| BEADED PLYWOOD PANELING. You can buy this 1/4-in.-thick paneling unfinished, or with a clear painted finish. Get a partial sheet (2x4 or 4x4) if you're planning to make just one shelf unit.

2| 1/2-IN. BIRCH PLYWOOD. You can buy a half sheet (4x4), which will be more than adequate for sides and shelves.

3| BEADED SCREEN MOLDING. This delicate molding is 3/4 in. wide and about 1/4 in. thick. You'll need about 8 ft.

4| LATTICE MOLDING. This square-edged trim is 1/4 in. thick and 1 1/4 in. wide. Make sure to buy straight stock.

5| CAP MOLDING. Different cap profiles are available. The one you choose should have a bottom edge around 1/4 in. thick, to combine well with the beaded screen molding.

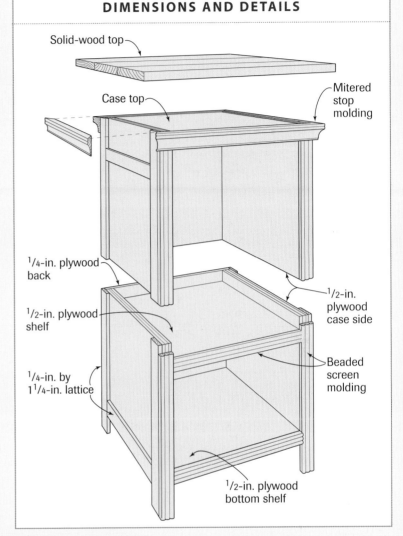

DIMENSIONS AND DETAILS

Solid-wood top

Case top

Mitered stop molding

1/4-in. plywood back

1/2-in. plywood shelf

1/4-in. by 1 1/4-in. lattice

1/2-in. plywood case side

Beaded screen molding

1/2-in. plywood bottom shelf

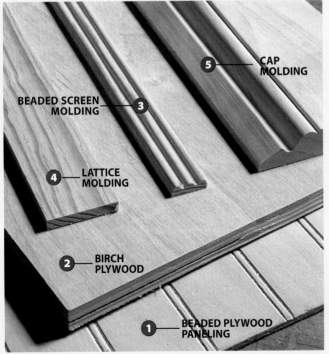

5 — CAP MOLDING

BEADED SCREEN MOLDING — 3

4 — LATTICE MOLDING

2 — BIRCH PLYWOOD

1 — BEADED PLYWOOD PANELING

OTHER STUFF

PRIMER & PAINT. Buy a quick-dry primer that works well on bare wood. For the finish coat, choose a good-quality acrylic semigloss paint. It's OK to use an interior paint unless your shelves are in a moist area. If this is the case, go with exterior enamel.

BRADS. Get a small box of 1 1/4-in. brads to use in assembling the case. You'll also need some 1/2-in. brads to attach the lattice molding.

WOOD GLUE & WOOD PUTTY. You'll need some yellow wood glue to attach the molding. The wood putty is for filling nail holes and any gaps that you don't want to show in the finished piece.

SANDPAPER. With a couple of sheets of 120-grit sandpaper, you'll be able to soften sharp corners, smooth out uneven areas, and get the wood set for finishing.

❶ **NEED A HAND?**

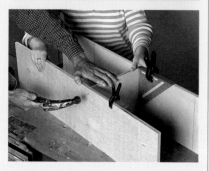

It's not easy to hold shelves right on their layout lines as you nail them in place. If you don't have a helper (or even if you do), get some alignment assistance from a couple of inexpensive squares that are held in place with spring clamps. These plastic squares cost around $2 apiece and come in handy for many layout and assembly jobs.

▶ **DO IT RIGHT**

Don't drive brads or finish nails all the way flush with the wood surface because you might mar the wood with a hammer blow. Instead, let the head of the nail stand proud, then "set" it using a nail set. The resulting hole is then filled with wood putty and sanded smooth.

Building the Case

1 **CUT THE SIDES & SHELVES TO WIDTH.** After marking the cutline on the plywood, clamp a straightedge guide to the panel. Align the straightedge parallel to the cutline to guide the base of your saw and keep the blade exactly on the cutline. Adjust the saw's cutting depth ⅛ in. greater than the material thickness. Make the cut by guiding the base of the saw against the straightedge.

2 **CUT THE SIDES & SHELVES TO LENGTH.** A good way to make sure your sides are identical is to cut them at the same time, with the two boards you cut to width (step 1) stacked together. Guide the base of your saw against a straightedge that's positioned for a square cut. Use the same strategy to cut shelves.

3 **MARK SHELF LOCATIONS WITH A SQUARE & PENCIL.** Put the sides together on a flat work surface. Using your tape measure, locate where shelves will fit on the sides. Then mark shelf lines across both sides, using the framing square to keep your lines true.

4 **GET IT TOGETHER!** Nail the sides to the shelves with 1¼-in. brads. Three nails per connection should do it. To make nailing easier, you can predrill holes in the sides, using a 1/16-in.-dia. bit. Mark pencil lines on outside faces to keep nails centered in shelf edges.

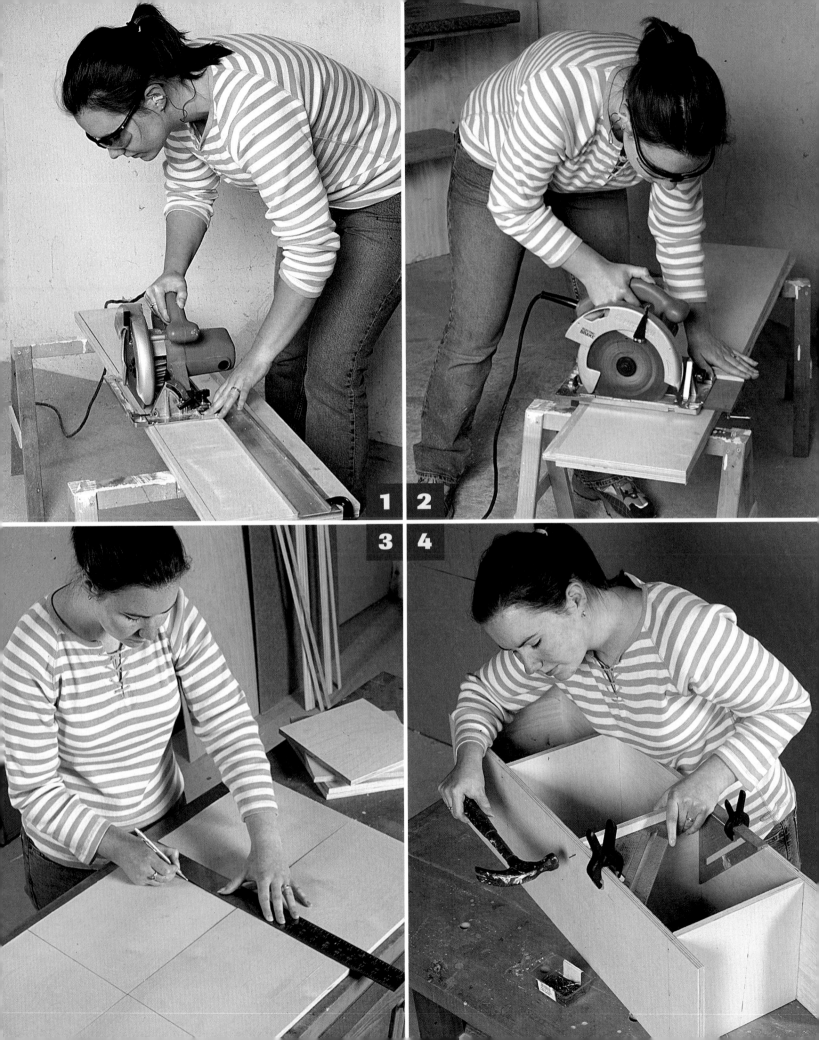

Adding Trim

5 **CUT OUT THE LEGS.** The cutout area on the bottom of each side follows the edge lines for the stiles and bottom rail (see the drawing on p. 47). Use a jigsaw or coping saw to make the cutout in each side.

6 **INSTALL THE STILES.** Using your miter box, cut each stile to exact length. Spread some glue along the back of each piece, and nail it to the side with ½-in. brads. Space brads 8 in. to 10 in. apart. Remember that the back edge of each rear stile needs to overhang the back of the case by ¼ in. This creates a recess where the back of the case will fit.

7 **INSTALL THE RAILS.** Cut the top and bottom rails to fit snugly between the stiles. If your leg cutout (step 5) was less than perfect, here's your chance to hide the error. Locate the bottom rail so that it covers the uneven edge of the cutout.

8 **MAKE YOUR FIRST MITER CUT.** The cap molding goes on next, around the top of the case. There are four cap pieces, and they need to meet each other with precisely cut miter joints. You can get started by making a 45-degree miter cut on one end of a length of cap molding. Hold the molding firmly against the bottom and back of the miter box and cut with a smooth, steady stroke.

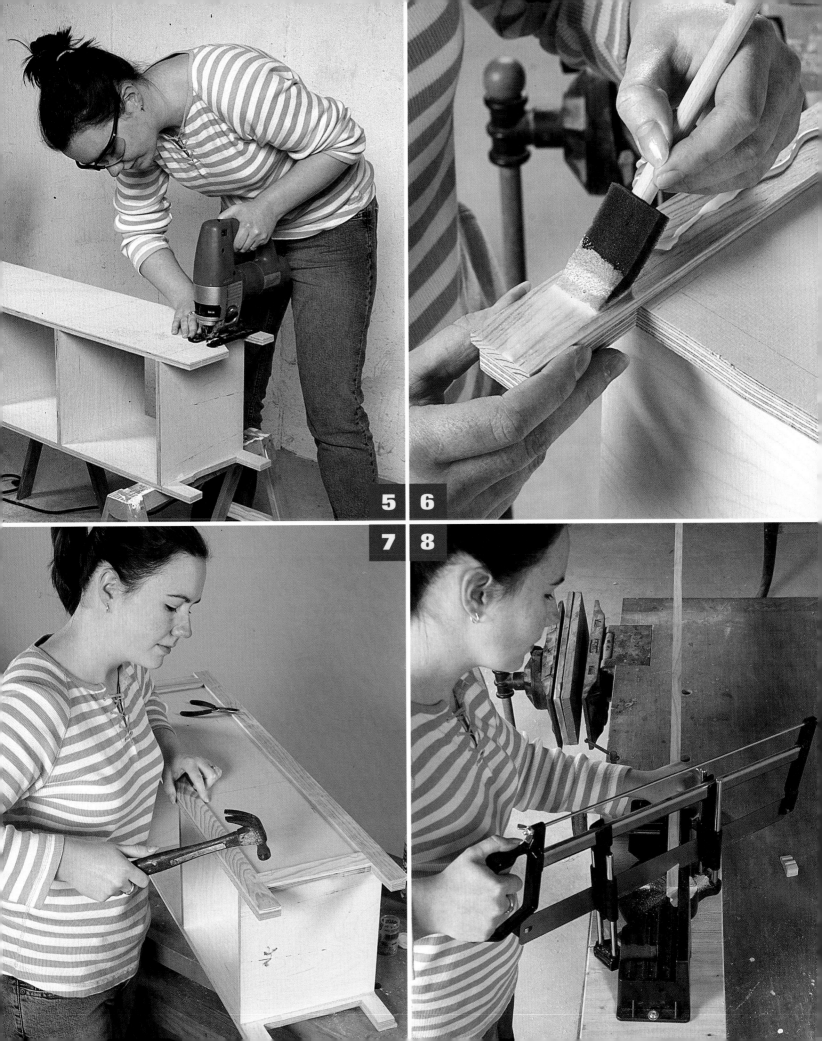

5 6
7 8

Mitered Molding

9 **MARK THE OPPOSITE MITER.** After mitering one end of the molding (step 8), cut the first piece a couple of inches longer than it needs

to be to fit across the front of the case. Then hold the piece on the case and mark the location of the opposite miter. Use a combination square to lay out the miter cut along the top edge of the molding. Cut the miter, then tack the piece to the case with a couple of 1¼ in. brads.

10 **MITER, MARK & CUT THE REMAINING PIECES.** Work your way around the top of the case by mitering one end of each piece, holding it in its installed position, and then marking the opposite end for the next miter cut. When both miters have been cut, glue and nail the piece in place.

11 **CUT & INSTALL THE BACK MOLDING LAST.** This piece of molding doesn't fit against the stile trim like the other pieces. Install it by gluing and nailing the miter joints together. Make sure to predrill the nail holes to avoid splitting the wood.

12 **INSTALL THE BEADED MOLDING.** Two long pieces cover the front edges of the sides; short pieces cover the front edges of the shelves. Using your miter box, cut all these parts to size. Spread glue on the back of one side piece, and install it by driving a ½-in. brad

through the center bead every 10 in. or so. Install the shelf pieces next, followed by the remaining side piece.

9 10
11 12

Sand & Finish

13 **FILL & SAND.** Fill the holes with wood putty. Go ahead and overfill, so you can sand the putty even with the wood after it dries. Use 120-grit sandpaper to smooth rough or uneven areas and to soften any sharp corners on the pine top.

14 **CUT THE TOP & BACK, THEN PAINT EVERYTHING.** Size the top to overhang the cap molding by ½ in. on all sides. Choose a flat, smooth piece of pine for the top, or glue two good pieces together. Cut the back from a sheet of ¼-in. beaded paneling. It should fit between the two rear stiles, resting evenly on the back edges of the case. You'll want to apply primer and finish coats on all surfaces of the case, back and top.

Painting the case before attaching the back makes the job much easier. Let the primer coat dry thoroughly, then smooth out any drips or rough areas with some 220-grit sandpaper. Brush the primed and sanded surface clean before applying the finish coat.

15 **ATTACH THE TOP.** The top's four installation screws are hidden because you drive them from underneath the case top. Put the top and case upside-down on the workbench, center the case on the top, and drill a pilot hole for a 1¼-in. screw near each corner. Don't worry if screw holes are driven at a slight angle. Drive screws through the case top and into the pine top. Use a long Phillips-head bit in your drill, as shown in the photo.

16 **PUT ON THE BACK.** The top edge of the back will slide under the bottom edge of the cap molding. Nail through the back and into the back edges of the sides and shelves, spacing nails about 10 in. apart. White-colored paneling nails are good to use because the heads blend in nicely with the painted back.

13 14

15 16

When you've built one set of these shelves, it's a sure bet you can build others. Duplicate the dimensions or details if you want an identical unit. This will give you a pair of pedestals that can support a glass top. Another option is to change the dimensions to suit your storage needs or your sense of style. Go shorter, taller, deeper, or broader, depending on the space you want to fill. Another reason to change project dimensions is because you want the shelf space to hold storage baskets or other containers. Changing the dimensions won't alter the construction sequence, so you can follow the same steps. If you want to build a bookcase with adjustable shelves, see the project that begins on page 26. How about finishing details?

A short column makes a fine end table. White paint can really pop out against a bold-colored wall or blend in with white walls.

The base on this project has a "soldier blue" milk paint finish. The contrasting top is pine that has been darkened with a mahogany stain and then coated with polyurethane varnish.

Some points on painting: Semi-gloss enamel is the best choice if your shelves will be used in the bathroom. No matter where this project goes, it's smart to give the top an extra coat of paint for added durability.

Closet Makeover

Put an end to messy, inefficient closets with **MODULAR COMPONENTS** you can customize to suit your needs

ES, THERE ARE COMPANIES THAT SPECIALIZE in closet makeovers. But this is a project you can do on your own, thanks to the wide range of closet-organizer systems available. The wood-slat system we installed is just one of your options. Wire components and other systems even include drawers and cabinets (see p. 68). No matter what components you choose, you'll find that many of the installation details are the same. The work usually begins with a total closet cleanout; you'll have to remove the old cleats, shelves, and poles. When your makeover is complete, you can expect your closet's storage capacity to increase by 50% to 75%. That's a great incentive to get started.

BACK TO BARE WALLS   LAY OUT   ASSEMBLE   ATTACH THE RAILS

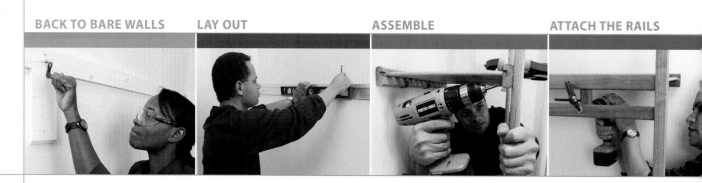

Cut down on your stair time by putting your tools and gear in a tool bucket or toolbox and getting them upstairs in a single trip.

A short, toolbox-size handsaw is a very handy tool to have in your arsenal. It's much easier to carry around than a full-size saw, and it cuts just as well.

Tools & Gear

DROP CLOTH. Protect carpets and simplify cleanup by laying down a canvas drop cloth before you start.

HAMMER & PRYBARS. You'll need these tools to remove the wood cleats that support the old shelf and clothes pole. A small "cat's paw" prybar designed for pulling nails is helpful; so is a larger prybar, sometimes called a "trim bar."

TAPING KNIVES. You can expect some damage to closet walls from removing the cleats and shelf. If you're careful, the only damage from removing your old closet system will be small nail holes that you can fill with spackling compound. Use the wide knife to hold a working quantity of compound and as an edge to clean the smaller blade that applies it.

ROLLER, BRUSH & TRAY. It's smart to repaint the closet before you begin to install the new components. Get a 3-in. synthetic brush to cut in and to paint any trim and a 9-in. roller (with $1/2$-in. nap cover) to paint the walls.

CORDLESS DRILL/DRIVER. Can you use a regular screwdriver? Sure. But a cordless drill will get the job done a lot faster.

DRILL ACCESSORIES. You'll need a quick-change bit holder, a #2 Phillips-head bit, a combination countersink/counterbore bit, and two small bits: $1/32$-in. and $5/16$-in.

TAPE MEASURE. A 16-ft. or 20-ft. model with a 1-in.-wide blade is stiff enough to extend several feet without support, making one-person measuring a breeze.

SAW. There's very little cutting, so a toolbox handsaw will do.

RAFTER SQUARE. Use this to mark square cuts and when cutting shelves.

QUICK CLAMPS. These lightweight bar clamps have padded jaws, so they won't damage your closet components; they're also easy to operate with one hand—a great advantage if you're working alone.

LEVEL. This will help you mark level lines throughout the closet to guide your installation.

What to Buy

1| JOINT COMPOUND. A gallon of "lightweight" joint compound or even a small container of spackling compound will do.

2| SANDING SPONGE. You just need a fine-grit one for this project. It lasts a long time, it's washable, and it's stiff enough to smooth flat surfaces yet flexible enough to conform to irregular ones.

3| CLOSET SYSTEM & HARDWARE. Systems are available in wire, melamine, and wood. Many systems offer drawers and easily adjustable shelves and rods. You can buy components separately or in kit form. Kits are often sold according to closet size and come in many configurations. Most kits come with hardware, but be sure to check the box.

4| WALL PAINT. Measure the area to be covered. You might get by with a quart of interior latex paint.

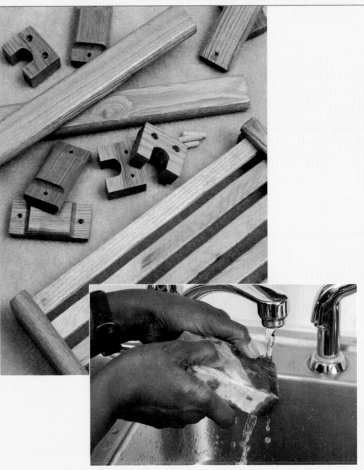

DESIGNING YOUR NEW CLOSET

Start by determining your needs. Chances are you'll want hang-up space for long clothes, such as dresses, as well as shorter items, such as shirts. You'll also need to store shoes and boots. And you may want to include shelves or drawers for folded items and accessories. Next, measure your closet (be sure to remove anything in the closet that might hamper measuring). Choose a system that best suits your needs and budget. Manufacturers offer a range of design help, from simply stating the heights required for rods to elaborate online planning programs that give you a materials list, pricing, and detailed step-by-step instructions. The larger your space or the more varied your needs, the more help you may appreciate, but honestly, most planning can be easily done on graph paper. Just record your measurements and start playing with fitting the components you want. It's nice to have it all on paper during installation so you can remind yourself just where you thought everything would fit.

This very small nail puller has a small pointed head with sharp jaws to dig in and pull small finishing nails with very little damage to wood. It is also available in larger sizes for larger nails.

SAFETY FIRST

When doing demolition work, always pull nails from old boards immediately to avoid puncture wounds. A pair of "nippers" makes it easy to pull finishing nails out from the back.

Get a Fresh Start

1 **REMOVE THE EXISTING ROD & SHELF.** Protect floors with a drop cloth. Lift out the rod and unscrew its brackets. If the shelf is attached to the cleat with screws, remove them. If it's nailed, tap up on the shelf with a hammer.

2 **REMOVE THE SHELF CLEATS.** Look for dimples that indicate fastener locations. Drive the tip of a prybar into the wood and over the head of the nail to pry it out. If you can't find the nail heads, pry cleats loose using your hammer and a prybar.

3 **SPACKLE & SAND.** Spread a thin coat of joint compound over damaged areas. Sand your patched areas smooth when the compound has dried completely—it turns bright white. Make a second application if necessary.

4 **PAINT.** Apply a fresh coat of wall paint. (You might want to brighten up the ceiling now, too.) Use a paintbrush to cut in a 2-in.-wide border at the ceiling and along inside corners, door casing, and baseboard molding. Then use a paint roller to fill in the rest.

1 **2**
3 **4**

You'll find it easier to attach the wooden garment rail hangers to the shelves before installing the shelves.

Bore a countersunk pilot hole in the back of the shelf rail with a combination bit (see p. 13) at an angle that lets you use a drill/driver to drive the screw.

Install the Closet System

5 **MARK THE HEIGHT.** Figure out how high you want the shelf, then lightly pencil a level line on the closet walls at the desired height. Use a level as a guide.

6 **ATTACH THE HOOKS.** Mark shelf-hook locations along the line, evenly spaced and no more than 16 in. apart. (The manufacturer's directions may have specific information about spacing.) If attaching the hook into a stud, use a screw. If there is no stud, predrill a $\frac{5}{16}$-in.-dia. hole, then drive in a winged hollow wall anchor.

7 **INSTALL AN END SUPPORT.** Put the shelf into the mounting hooks, and while holding it level, position an end bracket and mark its location on the side wall. Then remove the shelf and install the brackets, using mounting hooks as in the previous step.

8 **INSTALL THE SHELVES.** After first attaching rail support cleats (see DO IT NOW at left), place the shelf in its supports, level it, and clamp the shelf's front rail to a freestanding vertical support. Use a level to make sure the vertical support is plumb. Then fasten the shelf front rail to the vertical support with supplied screws. Make sure to drill a pilot hole for each screw to avoid splitting the wood.

+ WHAT CAN GO WRONG

If you drill the pilot holes for the garment rail too deep, you may drill through the face of the garment rail. To avoid this, attach a depth stop to the bit as shown, or simply wrap masking tape around the bit at the point you want to stop drilling.

More Shelves & a Rod

9 **INSTALL THE CENTER SHELVES.** Assemble and position the second vertical support. Then install your first center shelf by first anchoring shelf hooks to the wall (steps 5 and 6), then clamping and screwing the shelf's front rail to the vertical supports. Repeat this procedure to install all remaining center shelves.

10 **CUT THE LAST SHELF.** Cut the remaining shelf to fit between the vertical support and the other side wall. To make a smooth, accurate cut, set the shelf on a pair of 2x4s and guide the blade of your handsaw against a straightedged board held square across the shelf.

11 **INSTALL THE LAST SHELF.** Fasten shelf hooks to the wall and mount the end support (steps 5, 6, and 7) to install the last shelf or shelves. Then, after all shelves are installed, drive a screw through each rear-support bracket and into the shelf it supports.

12 **ATTACH THE GARMENT RAILS.** Measure and cut the garment rails with a handsaw. Clamp the garment rail to the hangers that you attached to the shelf before you installed it (step 8). Drive a screw through the predrilled hole in the cleat and into the rail. Vacuum up, and you're ready to hang clothes!

9 10
11 12

Peaceful mornings at last.

An organized, accessible closet is more than a space- and time-saver, it's a peacemaker, too. Imagine calm mornings with everything at your fingertips instead of the usual frantic search through too-deep drawers or crammed closets. Such systems are not only easy to build but also easy on the eyes and accommodating to changes in size, season, or owner. No space goes wasted—tuck in another shelf or rearrange clothes poles to suit.

Closet components can be a gadget-lover's dream. Every piece has a function; this slide-out rod can hold a stack of jackets or tomorrow morning's outfit.

A makeover can double the usefulness of a walk-in closet. This stacking basket system allows clothes to be instantly visible and also provides a countertop.

Don't shortsheet your linens when redoing closets. These wire components allow linens to breathe and can be adjusted to accommodate various stack sizes.

A coated wire closet system is easy to install and far sturdier than its lightweight lines suggest. You can choose from many configurations and components.

There are three secrets to success in a kid's closet: lots of light, durable construction, and adjustable heights for shelves and clothes poles.

With its cherry veneer finish, this system is too handsome to cover up and provides enough space for two people.

Wood-veneered shelves and drawers add elegance to this modular system. All components are mounted on slotted vertical standards that are screwed to the wall. The photo at right shows another configuration that's possible in the same amount of space.

A sunny, open storage niche is painted a solid yellow to complement wallpaper. As the little girl grows, it's easy to change clothes rod heights as well as wall colors.

If you like to look at your clothes and favor "grab-and-go" convenience, try an open closet arrangement like this.

Stronger than Dirt

Conquer laundry room clutter with **WIRE SHELVES & CABINETS** you can assemble and install yourself

THIS CABINET AND SHELF SOLUTION to laundry room clutter just might change your attitude about getting your clothes clean. Check out the cabinet part of this project—it can be a great storage solution outside the laundry room, too. "Ready-to-assemble" cabinets cost a fraction of what you'd pay for fully assembled versions, and you'll find base and wall cabinet sizes to fit any space. Wire shelves take up where cabinets leave off, giving you a storage system that's clean looking, accessible, and easy to customize with loads of accessories. You'll save enough by tackling this project yourself to buy a compact stereo—a helpful accessory in any laundry room.

| WALL CABINETS | BASE CABINET BASICS | HANG WIRE SHELVES | ADD END SUPPORTS |

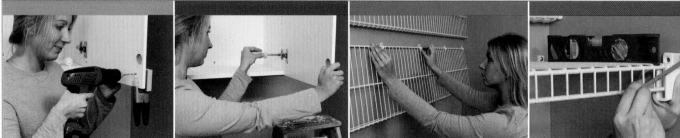

⬢ LINGO

The hinges used on these cabinets are called concealed hinges or Euro hinges. Despite their complex appearance, these hinges are easy to install. And they're easy to adjust, too. Just by turning an adjustment screw, you can fine-tune the alignment of a door without having to remove it first.

✱ UPGRADE

Typically the hinges that come with ready-to-assemble cabinets will only allow doors to open just over 90 degrees. If that is a problem, you can replace them with a style that allows the doors to open up to 180 degrees. And check out the roll-out trays on p. 88 if you want to upgrade your laundry room cabinets.

Tools & Gear

DRILL/DRIVER. As it is for so many projects today, the drill/driver—and a few basic accessories such as a magnetic bit holder—is a key tool for both of these projects.

HAMMER & SCREWDRIVER. Some assembly still requires an old-fashioned hammer and screwdriver, in this case a 16-oz. nail hammer and #2 Phillips driver.

QUICK CLAMP. A padded clamp won't harm cabinet finishes.

LEVELS. To get cabinets and shelves installed correctly, you'll need a small "torpedo" level and a 2-ft. or 4-ft. level. A laser level can take the place of these larger levels.

CIRCULAR SAW. If you plan to include a counter-top, you'll need a circular saw to cut it.

SAWHORSES & 2x4s. To cut your countertop, you'll need to support it solidly with 2x4s laid across a pair of sawhorses.

STUD FINDER. You'll need a stud finder so you can find and mark studs before installation.

TAPE MEASURE. You'll use a tape measure to mark locations for the screws and drywall anchors.

COOL TOOL

This compact laser level can be attached to the wall and project a level line to position shelves or mounting hardware. It can also be used to project plumb lines and other straight layout lines.

What to Buy

1 | BASE & WALL CABINETS. Your local home center will have a good selection of "ready-to-assemble" (RTA) cabinets available. Size your cabinets to fit the space in your laundry room. Cabinets will come with either a white melamine or wood-grain finish. Different door styles may also be available.

2 | LAMINATE COUNTERTOP. Pick a laminate finish from the countertops stocked at your home center, or order a special countertop. Buying a stock countertop will save you money, but you'll probably have to cut it to length. (See the sidebar below.) Buy an end trim kit with a matching laminate finish.

3 | SHIM PACK. Since floor and wall surfaces aren't always flat, level, and plumb, it's good to have a pack of tapered shims handy to "true up" your cabinets when you install them.

4 | WIRE SHELVING & HARDWARE. Measure the space where you plan to install your wire shelves, and have the shelves cut to length where you buy them. You'll also need braces, end caps, mounting clips, and other hardware. Consult with your dealer or read the manufacturer's guidelines to determine what hardware to buy.

5 | CAULK & GLUE. You'll need wood glue for cabinet assembly and some latex caulk to fill gaps between the wall and the countertop or cabinet.

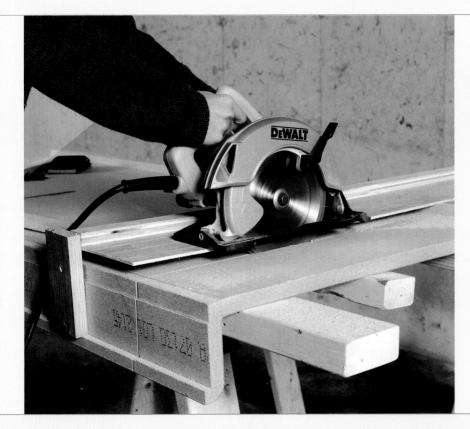

DO IT RIGHT

Cutting a laminate countertop to fit your base cabinet isn't as difficult as it seems. Get set by supporting the C-top upside-down on some 2x4s set across sawhorses. Put a finish-cutting blade in your circular saw, and set up a straightedge guide for your saw. Insert scrap-wood filler strips under the straightedge to create a flat cutting surface. Make the long cut first, across the bottom of the countertop. Then set up and cut the backsplash. Smooth the cut surface with some 120-grit sandpaper wrapped around a sanding block.

▶ DO IT RIGHT

To square the cabinet: Measure the diagonals from corner to corner and rack the case by pushing or tapping on the corner where the measurements need to shorten slightly. You're square when diagonal measurements are equal.

✧ DO IT NOW

After you locate the studs where your cabinet will be installed, attach a temporary cleat to support the cabinet along its bottom edge while you install it. Use your tape measure to transfer the stud locations to the mounting cleats inside of the cabinet, then drill clearance holes for your installation screws.

✛ WHAT CAN GO WRONG

If you drill holes for door handles without clamping on a backer board, the drill can splinter the face as it exits. This is particularly true for wood-veneered cabinets.

Installing a Wall Cabinet

1 **ASSEMBLE THE CASE.** Assemble the case with the provided fasteners. Square the case (see DO IT RIGHT at left) before attaching the back with glue and nails. Drill pilot holes for these nails to make them easier to drive.

2 **HANG THE CABINET.** Attach a temporary cleat to the wall with drywall screws to support the cabinet weight and prepare the cabinet (see DO IT NOW at left). Using a stud finder, mark the studs. Position the cabinet and drive #10 x 2½-in. cabinet screws through the mounting cleats and into each stud. If you need to join two cabinets together, follow the manufacturer's instructions for doing so.

3 **INSTALL THE DOORS.** Each hinge has two parts. One fastens to the door; the other fastens to the side of the cabinet. Install both halves of each hinge. To mount the door, slide the hinge parts together and tighten the mounting screw. Close both doors to check for proper alignment. Turn the adjusting screws as explained in the manufacturer's directions to get each door aligned correctly.

4 **INSTALL THE SHELVES & KNOBS.** Clamp a block of wood to the face of the door and finish drilling the holes for door handles. Insert the mounting screws, then install the handles. Figure out what shelf heights will work best for you, then insert shelf supports into the holes in the cabinet sides. Install your shelves, and start making the most of your new storage space.

∴ DO IT NOW

To make your cabinet fit against the wall, you'll probably need to notch the bottom of each side to fit over baseboard trim. Position the cabinet near the wall and use a compass as shown to transfer the profile of the base trim to the side of the cabinet. Make the cut with a jigsaw.

✛ WHAT CAN GO WRONG

When doing assembly and installation work in your laundry room, it's easy to damage the floor or even the finishes on your washer and dryer. To avoid this, lay down a protective layer of cardboard. You'll have plenty from the cartons that contain your cabinets.

Base Cabinet Basics

5 **ASSEMBLE THE CASE.** Recruit a helper and you'll have an easier time handling heavy case pieces. Get set for assembly by placing one case side flat on the floor. Tap assembly hardware and wood dowels (use glue on the dowels) into the case sides and rails as shown on the manufacturer's directions. Insert the rails into one, slide in the back as shown, then attach the other side. Tighten all connecters using a screwdriver by hand; don't use a drill/driver.

6 **SET THE CABINET.** Level the cabinet by inserting shims under and behind it as necessary. If there is base molding, notch the back of the cabinet to fit over it using a jigsaw (see DO IT NOW at left). Bore clearance holes through the mounting rail at two stud locations, and drive in #10 x 2½-in. screws to fasten the cabinet to the wall. Cut off excess shim material using a utility knife.

7 **PREPARE THE COUNTERTOP.** Cut the countertop to the length you need (see DO IT RIGHT on p. 75). Then attach the filler pieces (in your end cap kit) with glue and ¾-in. brads. Use a household iron to adhere each iron-on end cap. Take the sharp edge off with a rubber sanding block.

8 **ATTACH THE TOP.** The countertop is usually installed with plastic tabs that are included with other assembly hardware. Screw the tab to the top of the cabinet case first, following the manufacturer's directions. Then position the countertop, duck inside the case, and drive a screw up through each tab and into the underside of the top. It's smart to drill pilot holes for these screws.

DO IT NOW

Drill a clearance hole for a knob (or two holes for a pull) in each drawer front before you attach it to the drawer case. Use a backer board as you did for the doors (see step 9) to prevent damage as the drill penetrates the face.

DO IT RIGHT

Don't remove the shims after installation. Instead, use a sharp utility knife to cut off the excess. It's safer to make several passes than to press too hard.

Doors & Drawer

9 **INSTALL THE DOORS.** Fasten the hinge halves to the door and cabinet, using the screws included in your cabinet's hardware package. Mount the door by sliding the hinge parts together and tightening the mounting screw. Close both doors to check for proper alignment. Turn the adjusting screws to fine-tune door alignment until both doors hang straight and evenly.

10 **ASSEMBLE THE DRAWER.** Like the cabinet case, the drawer is assembled from precut parts. Join the front, bottom, and back to the sides, following the manufacturer's instructions. Finish assembling the drawer case by driving screws at designated locations. Then insert the drawer into the cabinet.

11 **ATTACH THE DRAWER FRONTS.** This drawer has two fronts that need to be screwed to the front of the drawer case. Install knobs or pulls as shown in step 4 before you attach the drawer fronts, using predrilled holes and the provided screws. Tighten the screws fully after you check and adjust the alignment of both drawer fronts when the drawer is closed.

12 **FILL GAPS WITH CAULK OR TRIM.** Don't worry if you find gaps between the cabinet and the wall or floor. Use latex caulk to fill gaps less than about ⅛ in. wide. For large gaps, simply cut and attach a small molding.

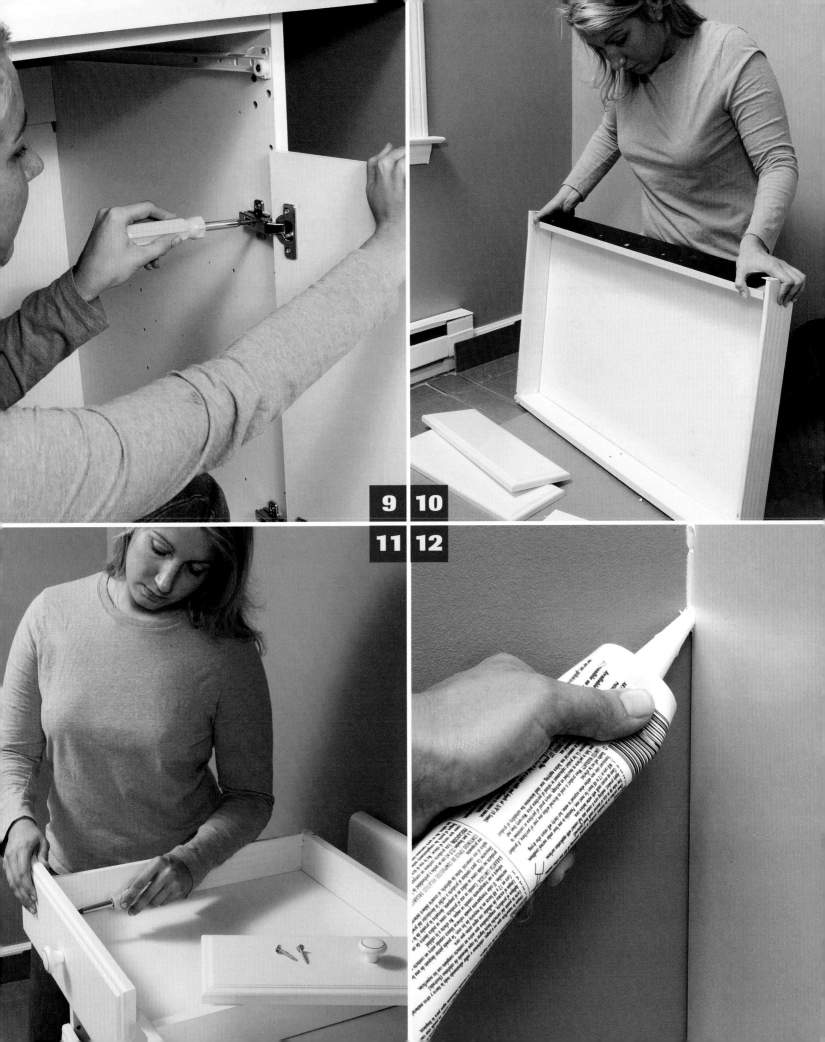

9 **10**

11 **12**

Installing Wire Shelving

13 **LOCATE YOUR SHELVES.** Mark a level line on the wall where each shelf will be installed. If you don't have a laser level, a regular 2-ft. or 4-ft. level will work fine. Mark an anchor location every 12 in. along each shelf line. Drill a ¼-in.-dia. hole through the drywall at each mark.

14 **INSTALL A SHELF.** Tap a drywall anchor into each hole and tighten its screw with your drill/driver, being careful not to overdrive the screw. Hook the back rail of the shelf over the anchors, and press at each anchor to snap the back rail in place.

15 **INSTALL AN END BRACKET.** Placing a torpedo level across the top of a shelf will enable you to keep it level. With the shelf held this way, position the end bracket to mark its mounting holes. Drill ¼-in.-dia. holes at your marks and install the bracket by tapping in the anchors and then driving the screws.

16 **ADD DIAGONAL BRACES.** Add diagonal braces at every other wall-anchor location. Hook the bracket on the front of the shelf and press the other end against the wall to mark its mounting hole. Drill a ¼-in.-dia. hole and install a drywall anchor. Then reposition the bracket and screw it to the anchor. Use this same installation sequence for every shelf. Nice work. Now you're ready to load 'em up!

13 14
15 16

Storage solutions abound for laundry rooms. To find out what's right for you, start by thinking about what should be visible and accessible, and what you'd rather store in a cabinet. Give yourself space for laundry baskets, clothes poles, and other essential elements. Durable components are important in this hard-working room. Don't forget about bright colors and good lighting to keep the mood upbeat.

Chrome-plated standards and slotted steel shelves look sharp in a lavender laundry room with white appliances and baskets.

Perforated wall panels work like pegboard but come with a durable factory-applied finish. Shelf support brackets, hooks, plastic bins, and clothes-pole supports are easy to install and reposition.

A corner in a mudroom or bathroom is a perfect spot for fitting in a skinny laundry-storage system. Basket drawers let air circulate around towels and dirty laundry.

Make your washer and dryer feel like built-in kitchen appliances by surrounding them with cabinets. Laminate-covered cabinets are inexpensive, durable, and easy to keep clean.

Although these rugged-looking cabinets are most often used in garage and workshop spaces, their durable, no-nonsense design makes a style statement in this laundry room.

Tuck a storage system into a closet with a stacked washer-dryer unit and you have an instant laundry room that's easily concealed by handsome bifold doors.

For a storage strategy that's fast, flexible, and inexpensive, it's hard to beat this combination of medium-duty shelving standards and plastic-coated wire shelving.

Who would guess that behind these handsome sliding doors is a small but serviceable laundry space? Since the washer and dryer are both front-loading models, a large countertop could be installed, creating ample storage and folding space.

Smarter Cabinets

Adding SLIDE-OUT TRAYS to your cabinets increases storage space & saves your back, too

I T'S TIME TO TEACH YOUR OLD CABINETS SOME NEW TRICKS. Pull-out trays have become standard equipment on expensive kitchen cabinets, but you don't have to buy new cabinets to enjoy this back-saving feature. In fact, you can add two or more trays to existing cabinets for less than $30. So if you're tired of getting down on your hands and knees to retrieve cooking gear from your cabinets, this project is just the ticket. You'll not only save time when you need to put your hands on pots and pans, you'll also be increasing a cabinet's storage space by 33%. Grab your tape measure, and let's get started.

MEASURE   **BUILD THE TRAYS**   **SLIDE HARDWARE**   **SMOOTH OPERATION**

◆ COOL TOOL

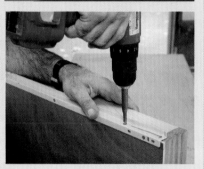

Chuck a Vix bit (aka self-centering bit) in your drill and you've got a foolproof way to drill pilot holes for hinge screws and other screws used to mount different types of hardware. The bit's tapered tip centers the drill bit exactly, so you don't have to worry about having your hardware shift out of position when you drive installation screws. Vix bits are usually sold in sets of three to fit a wide range of hinges and other hardware.

Tools & Gear

TAPE MEASURE. A tape with a wide, stiff blade is great for solo work because the blade will extend a long way without bending.

CIRCULAR SAW. For best results, make sure your saw has a sharp finish-cutting blade.

SQUARES. A large rafter square is good for general squaring and for guiding your circular saw. To mark and test for square on plywood panels, you'll need a framing square.

CLAMPS. A couple of 30-in.-long bar clamps will hold the glued drawer parts together for nailing. Smaller "quick clamps" help secure parts while you cut them to size.

CORDLESS DRILL/DRIVER. Check to make sure you've got both batteries charged before you begin.

DRILL ACCESSORIES. You'll work faster with a quick-change "drill-and-drive" bit set that includes a variety of bits.

SANDER OR SANDING BLOCK. A random-orbit sander will help you speed through the sanding and smoothing work required on this project. If you don't have one available, back up your sandpaper with a sanding block.

WHAT'S DIFFERENT?

Frameless (aka Euro-style) cabinets are built without face frames. If you're adding pull-out drawers to frameless cabinets, the drawer slide will be attached directly to the side of the cabinet. The cabinet door may interfere with the operation of the drawer, so this is something to check out before you begin. The easiest solution is to "pad out" the hinge side of the cabinet by attaching a 1x2 board to the cabinet side, beneath the drawer-slide hardware.

What to Buy

1 | ¼-IN. PLYWOOD. Birch plywood is usually your best bet. It finishes nicely, and it's stocked by most home centers and lumber yards.

2 | 1 X 3 STRIPS. Use straight, clear boards made from poplar, maple, or oak. Determine how much length to order by adding up the perimeter dimensions for every drawer you plan to build.

3 | NAILS. To assemble your trays, you'll need a box of 1-in. wire nails and a box of 4d finishing nails.

4 | GLUE. Yellow wood glue is what you need.

5 | SANDPAPER. Buy a five-pack of 80- and 120-grit sanding disks for your random-orbit sander or a few 9x11 sheets of these grits. Go with aluminum oxide sandpaper.

6 | DRAWER SLIDES. Drawer slide hardware comes in different sizes and styles. The slide hardware you want for this project is a "bottom-mount" slide in a 22-in. size. Buy a pair of drawer slides for each tray you plan to install.

7 | SLIDE BRACKETS. These brackets secure the back end of the drawer slide to the back of the cabinet. You'll need one bracket for each drawer slide. Frameless cabinets don't require brackets but may require boards to space them off the cabinet side (see WHAT'S DIFFERENT on the facing page).

8 | VARNISH. Two coats of clear varnish will protect your new drawers from stains and make them easier to clean. Use a water-based varnish in gloss or semigloss sheen.

9 | PAINTBRUSH. Get a good-quality, synthetic-bristle brush that's 2 in. to 3 in. wide.

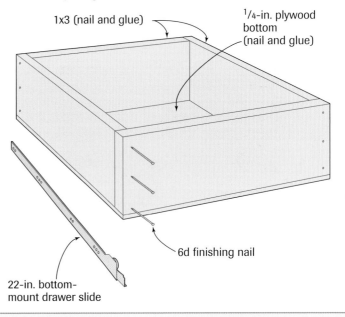

TRAY DETAILS

The dimensions of a roll-out tray depend on the size of the cabinet. Most base cabinets are deep enough to accommodate a 22-in. drawer slide. To get the finished width of your tray, subtract 1 in. from the width of the opening.

1x3 (nail and glue)

¼-in. plywood bottom (nail and glue)

6d finishing nail

22-in. bottom-mount drawer slide

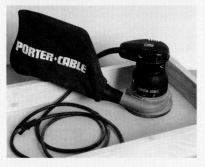
Making the Tray

1 **MEASURE THE CABINET.** Empty the cabinet and remove the shelf if it isn't permanently installed. Measure the width of the opening and the depth of the cabinet. A standard base cabinet will accept a 22-in.-deep tray. To determine the finished width of your tray, subtract *exactly* 1 in. from the width of the opening. This will give you the right clearance for a pair of drawer slides.

2 **CUT THE TRAY PARTS.** Mark and cut each tray bottom from a sheet of ¼-in. plywood. Use a straightedge guide for your circular saw, and measure carefully to make sure each tray has square corners. Cut the four tray sides from 1x3 strips (see DO IT RIGHT at left).

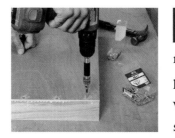

3 **ASSEMBLE THE TRAY.** Glue, clamp, and nail the sides together with 4d finishing nails. Use three nails at each joint, and drill pilot holes for the nails to avoid splitting the wood. As shown in the drawing on p. 91, make sure that the front piece covers the end grain of the two side pieces. Glue and nail the bottom to the sides with 1-in. brads spaced every 4 in.

4 **SAND & FINISH.** Do a thorough job of sanding each tray, paying special attention to the front, which will be the most visible part. Vacuum up all dust before applying two or three coats of polyurethane varnish. As an alternative to clear finish, you can apply stain or semigloss trim paint.

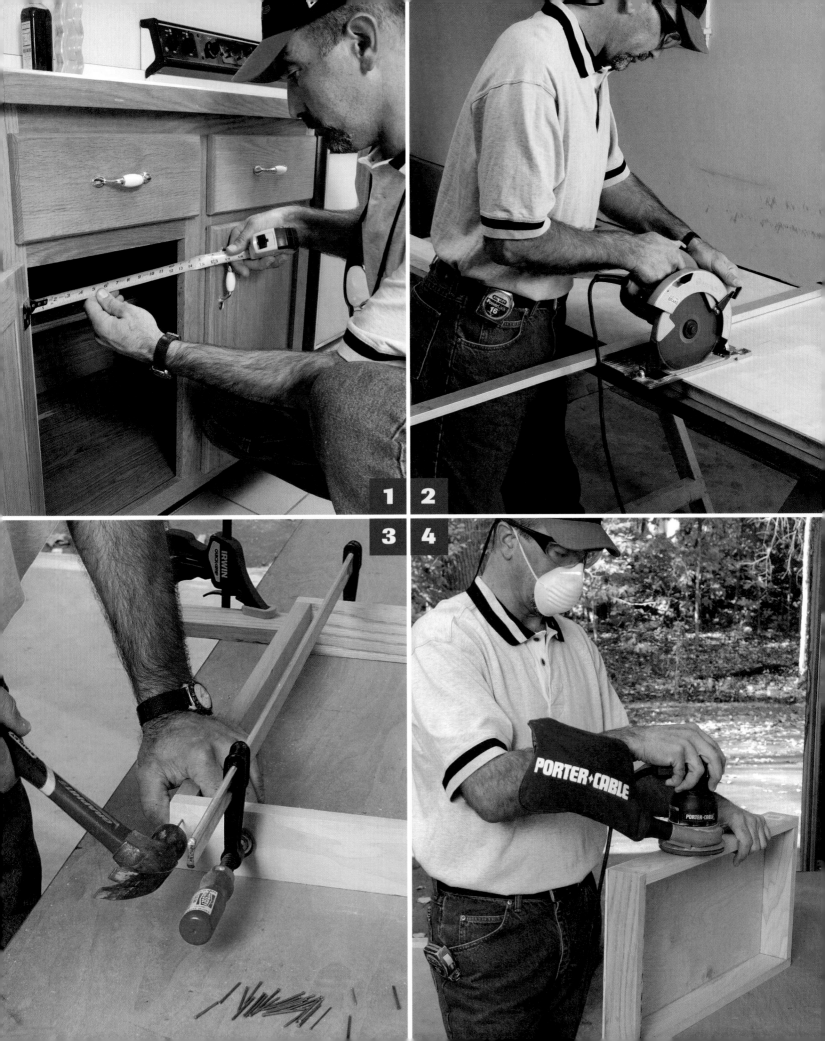

A magnetic torpedo level is just the right size for leveling drawer slides. And, because the slides are steel, your level will stay in place, freeing both hands to mark and drill slide installation holes.

Finishing & Installation

5 **FASTEN SLIDES TO THE TRAY.** Each of your bottom-mount drawer slides contains two parts—one that attaches to the drawer or tray, and another that is attached to the cabinet. Position the tray part of each slide on the bottom side edges of the tray, ⁵⁄₁₆ in. back from the front edge of the tray. Drill pilot holes, then drive the screws that came with your slide hardware.

6 **ATTACH THE REAR BRACKETS.** Insert the rear of the cabinet half of the slide into its rear mounting bracket. Then screw the bracket to the back of the cabinet, making sure that the slide is at the correct level. Repeat this procedure for the slide on the opposite side of the tray.

7 **ATTACH THE SLIDES TO THE FACE FRAME.** Level each slide and secure its front edge to the face frame according to the manufacturer's directions. The slides shown here need to be ¹⁄₁₆ in. back from the front edge of the face frame. For now, it's best to secure the front edge of each slide with just a single installation screw. Drill a pilot hole for the screw, then drive it.

8 **INSTALL YOUR TRAYS.** Insert the wheels on the rear of the tray's slide hardware into the track on the cabinet slides. If the slides mounted on the cabinet are level and parallel to each other—and we know they will be—remove the tray and drive the remaining slide-installation screws into the face frame. Great job. Now decide what to do with all the extra storage space!

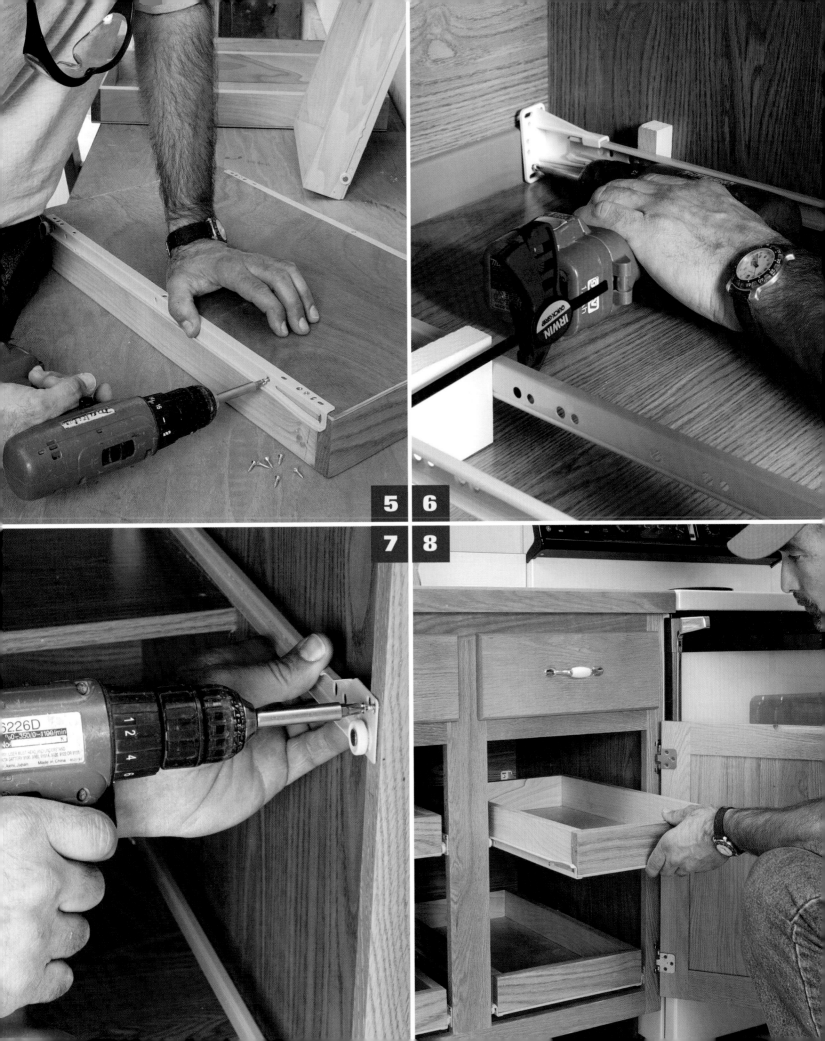

5

6

7

8

To exploit unused storage space in your sink cabinet, buy a tilt-out tray kit. Installing the tilt-out hardware and plastic tray gives you a great place to store sponges and scouring pads.

It looks expensive, but this pantry shelving system is affordable and easy to install, thanks to shelves and sides that are cut, drilled, and finished at the factory.

Cabinets can do more than just look good, especially if you take advantage of all the specialized hardware and storage components designed for kitchens. Although you may not be able to add more storage space, you can certainly make your existing space work with greater ease and efficiency. It's all about improving organization and accessibility.

Keeping a garbage pail under the sink can lead to traffic jams, so consider retrofitting a cabinet near the sink to hold pull-out bins for trash or recyclables.

Untangle family chaos by sorting and storing CD and DVD cases in specially designed drawer inserts. Just remember to put the CD back when you're done.

Many cooks find they'd rather pull out a drawer to find a pot than rummage on fixed shelves in base cabinets. Deep drawers, fitted with vertical dividers, improve accessibility and organization.

Installed several inches below your wall cabinets, this chrome rail helps to free up countertop space, with hooks and hangers that let you store a variety of items.

It's so much easier to clean up the kitchen when gear is stored on simple, inexpensive pull-out trays. Always lock such cabinets if small children are in your household.

An easy way to retrofit for a garbage bin is to remove interior shelves and hide a slide-out bin holder behind an existing cabinet door.

Okay, so where do you dry your dish towels? These pull-out rods make for neat, easy-access storage for linens you'd rather not see all the time.

Corkboard & Cubbies

Add COMPARTMENTS to a BULLETIN BOARD, & you've got a great way to get organized

A BULLETIN BOARD IS A GREAT WAY to keep tables and counter-tops clear of notices, notes, and the general flood of paper that easily accumulates around the house. Once you see how easy it is to make your own bulletin board, you'll wonder why you ever bought one. You'll save money by building your own, and you can make any size you want. Another bonus: The built-in cubby-holes turn this project into a capable organizer for bills, envelopes, stamps, pens, and other items. You might want to make more than one.

BUILD THE BOX   GLUE THE CORK   CASE IT   FINISH IT

✳ CORKBOARD&CUBBIES

▶ LINGO

A couple of specialized fasteners are needed for this project. Trim-head screws have small heads, like finishing nails, but they've got much more holding power. Paneling nails also hold better than regular nails, thanks to their ring-shank design.

Tools & Gear

HAMMER & NAIL SET. Glue will hold most of this project together, but you have to drive a few brads to hold parts in place while the glue sets. A tack hammer and a $1/32$-in. nail set will get the job done.

MITER BOX. To make precise crosscuts and miters, you'll need a miter box or a motorized chopsaw.

CORDLESS DRILL & SQUARE DRIVER. Charge up the battery on your drill, and get a driver bit that matches the small square recess in the trim-head screws you'll be using.

SMALL BITS. You'll need a $1/32$-in. drill bit to predrill nail holes in the cove molding. Get a $1/8$-in. bit for predrilling screw holes.

TAPE MEASURE. You'll need to measure your wood before you start cutting.

UTILITY KNIFE. Put a fresh blade in your knife so you can make straight, clean cuts in your corkboard.

SPRING CLAMPS. These clamps come in different sizes and do a great job of holding parts in place until glue sets or nails are driven. Clamps that can open to $1\frac{1}{2}$ in. or so are the most useful. You'll need at least four for this project.

PAINTBRUSHES. Get a disposable foam brush for spreading glue. To apply primer and paint, you'll need a good-quality trim brush that's $1\frac{1}{2}$ in. wide.

What to Buy

1 | ¼-IN. PLYWOOD. Depending on the size of the board you plan to build, you can buy either a 2x2 sheet or a 4x4 sheet. Check your panel carefully; it should be perfectly flat.

2 | 1X4 PINE. This lumber will actually measure ¾ in. thick and 3½ in. wide. Make sure to buy pieces that are clear, straight, and flat. Buy enough stock to make the shelf top, bottom, ends, and dividers.

3 | 2½-IN. COLONIAL CASING. "Casing" is any molding that's used around windows and doors. Feel free to substitute a different casing profile if you find one you like better.

4 | ¼-IN. X 1¾-IN. LATTICE MOLDING. This flat molding comes in different widths. Buy enough to extend around the edge of the bulletin board.

5 | ¾-IN. X ¾-IN. COVE MOLDING. This curved profile forms the outer edge of the shelf top. Buy extra, in case you miscut a miter or split the molding when installing it.

6 | CORKBOARD. This board is typically ¼ in. thick and is sold in rolls or squares. If your home center doesn't have corkboard in stock, try an office-supply store.

7 | SCREWS. Buy a small box of 1⅝-in. trim-head screws for assembling the cubbyhole unit. To hang the project on the wall, get two #8 x 2½-in. brass screws.

8 | BRADS & PANELING NAILS. You'll need ⅝-in. brads to attach the cove molding and ⅞-in. paneling nails to install the casing and back.

9 | DRYWALL ANCHORS. You'll need two 25-lb.-rated anchors to mount the bulletin board on the wall.

10 | WOOD GLUE. Regular yellow wood glue is what you need.

11 | WOOD PUTTY. Quick-drying "Plastic Wood" is a good choice for this project, but any type of wood putty will do.

12 | 150-GRIT SANDPAPER. You'll need a few sheets to do a thorough sanding job.

13 | PRIMER & PAINT. Semigloss interior enamel will give this project a durable, attractive finish. Apply it over a compatible primer.

CORKBOARD & CUBBYHOLE CONSTRUCTION

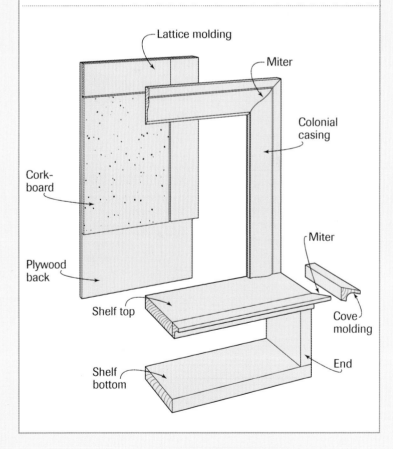

Lattice molding

Miter

Colonial casing

Cork-board

Plywood back

Shelf top

Miter

Cove molding

End

Shelf bottom

A sure way to cut two or more parts to identical size is to clamp a stop block on your miter box. Position the block so that it stops the end of the board to align the sawblade right on the cutline.

When you glue the lattice strips to the plywood (step 3), the strips can easily slip out of place. To prevent this, "tack" the strips in position with a couple of brads. You don't need to drive the brads all the way in—just deep enough to hold the lattice in position while clamps keep the parts together until the glue sets. Use a pair of pliers to pull the brads out after the glue sets.

Building It

1 **BUILD THE BOX.** The cubbyholes come first. Measure and mark the correct lengths for the shelf top, bottom, ends, and dividers, then use your miter box to cut them to size. If possible, recruit a helper to hold the top, bottom, and ends together while you predrill a pair of ⅛-in.-dia. holes at each joint. Use your cordless drill/driver and square-recess bit to join the top, bottom, and ends together with trim-head screws. Then screw the dividers in place.

2 **JOIN THE BOX TO THE PLYWOOD.** Spread a narrow bead of glue on the back edges of the cubbyhole assembly. Align the plywood back on the cubbyholes, then fasten it in place with paneling nails. Space the nails about 6 in. apart, and make sure to drive a nail into each end and divider.

3 **APPLY THE LATTICE STRIPS.** Cut the lattice strips to fit around the perimeter of the plywood, then glue them in place. Use spring clamps to hold the strips in place until the glue sets. Cut and fit the two side lattice pieces, then cut the top to fit between them.

4 **GLUE DOWN THE CORK.** Use a foam brush to spread an even coat of wood glue on the back of the cork tile. Then press the cork in place. Start with the bottom center square, then cut and fit the other tiles around it. Try for straight, gap-free joints where the cork panels butt against the shelf top and where panels meet each other. When all the cork is down, put some weight on the surface until the glue sets (about one hour).

Sand, Finish & Install

5 **ATTACH THE CASING & COVE.** Mark each piece of casing molding for its miter cut, and make the cut on the miter box. Tack the piece in place, then do the same for the next two pieces (see DO IT RIGHT at left). Repeat this mark, cut, and tack process for the cove molding that surrounds the shelf top. When the fit is right all around, glue and nail the pieces in place.

6 **SET, FILL & SAND.** Using your hammer and nail set, set all nail heads slightly below the wood surface. Apply wood filler, using the tip of a straight screwdriver. When the filler is dry, sand it flush with the wood surface, and give the entire project a thorough sanding to soften sharp edges and smooth irregularities.

7 **APPLY FINISH.** Mask off the bulletin-board surface with painter's tape or by tucking paper under the casing. Apply the primer and finish coats, following the directions on the can. To prevent the board from warping, give the back plywood surface a coat of primer.

8 **HANG, STICK & STORE.** The easy way to hang your project on the wall is with a pair of 2½-in.-long screws, driven near the top corners. Measure down 2½ in. from each corner, and drill a countersunk pilot hole near the outside edge of the casing, where the wood is thickest. Drive installation screws into drywall anchors. Nice job!

5

6

7

8

Chances are you've got notes, addresses, clever sayings, schedules, and other paper-based information scattered across your desk or table. Corkboards can keep these little bits of information pinned up and out of the way. But it's even nicer when a bulletin board gets teamed up with other storage and organizing tricks. That's why these cubbyhole and chalkboard combinations are so appealing.

This project variation gives equal space to corkboard and chalkboard, with cubbies beneath. You can create a chalkboard of any size using special chalkboard paint.

Cubbies overhead, cubbies down below—can there ever be too many? Where else to put stacks of phone books and other office necessities. The kitchen cubbies at right are strictly for a favorite collection of dishes and figurines.

Don't stop with corkboard and cubbyholes. Add some screw-in hooks along the bottom, and you've got an easy way to keep wayward keys under control.

This chalkboard and bulletin board combination includes a narrow ledge for holding chalk. A quirky paint job makes this framed project anything but square.

Literary Achievement

BEAUTIFUL BOOKCASES are expensive to buy, but you can build this one for less than $50

Y OU DON'T HAVE TO BE A BOOK LOVER to appreciate a nicely made bookcase. You get a generous amount of shelf space, adjustable shelf heights, and a showpiece that contributes to the style and ambience of a room. The nice thing about the bookcase we're building here is that the same step-by-step construction sequence will get you your own version in a size that suits your needs. You can make the shelves deeper to hold a stereo system, or the case shorter to fit beneath a window. There's only one problem with this project: Once you've finished it, you're going to have a hard time shelling out major money for a factory-made version.

| CUT THE PARTS | ASSEMBLE | ADD THE TRIM | SET THE SHELVES |

Plan your plywood cuts to minimize waste. Make a sketch to represent how you plan to cut all of the plywood pieces. In this case, that means making all rips (lengthwise cuts) first, then the crosscuts. The case parts to cut first are the sides, bottom, subtop, and back. The remaining parts can be cut to fit after the case is assembled.

❊ WHAT'S DIFFERENT?

To build the bookcase shown here, we covered the top's plywood edges with iron-on wood edgebanding. Another option is to glue solid-wood edging on top of the plywood edges. Solid-wood edging tends to be more durable. But it's also more conspicuous if the plywood is to be stained rather than painted.

Tools & Gear

SAWS. You'll need a circular saw and jigsaw to cut the case parts, and a hacksaw to cut the steel shelf standards.

BLOCK PLANE. This small plane does a good job of chamfering the edges of the shelves.

CUTTING GUIDES. It's more accurate and safer to use cutting guides with your circular saw. You'll need a large square to guide right-angled cuts and a shop-made panel-cutting guide for making long, straight cuts (see page 114).

DRILL/DRIVER & ACCESSORIES. To go with your cordless drill/driver, you'll need a combination bit, plus a #2 Phillips bit and a drill index.

CLAMPS. Assembling the case is easier if you have a couple of 36-in.-long bar clamps and several spring clamps.

RANDOM-ORBIT SANDER. This power sander will make it easy to smooth wood surfaces in preparation for painting or staining. You'll also find it helpful to have an inexpensive rubber block sander.

WHAT CAN GO WRONG

Glue that squeezes out of a joint can create problems if you plan to stain your project. The squeeze-out penetrates the wood and prevents stain from being absorbed evenly, creating a blotchy appearance. You can prevent this by applying glue evenly but sparingly and spreading it out with your finger or a small brush before joining parts together.

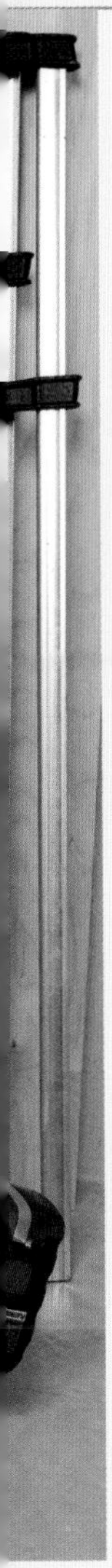

What to Buy

The lumber order described below is for a bookcase like the one shown here. The finished dimensions of the bookcase are 30 in. wide, 48 in. tall, and 10½ in. deep.

1 | PLYWOOD. Buy a 4x8 sheet of ¾-in. birch plywood for the case and shelves, and a half-sheet of ¼-in. beaded plywood paneling for the back.

2 | EDGEBANDING. The heat-activated adhesive backing on this thin wood edging lets you iron it on over plywood edges. Buy birch or maple banding.

3 | PILASTERS. This molding is often used for trim around windows and doors, but it works great on a bookcase, too. The pair of pilasters used on this case measure ⅝ in. thick and 3 in. wide.

4 | PINE OR POPLAR 1X4S. You'll use this wood for the skirt and top rail. Buy a 10-ft. board that's clear, straight, and flat.

5 | LATTICE MOLDING. Pick up two 8-ft. lengths of 1¼-in.-wide lattice molding to detail the sides of the case.

6 | BED MOLDING. This small, contoured molding is for the cornice just below the top. Get an 8-ft. length.

7 | STOP MOLDING. This square-edged stock is for edging the shelves. Buy a 6-ft. length of the ⅜-in. x 1-in. molding.

8 | FASTENERS. Buy some coarse-thread drywall screws in lengths of 2¼ in. and 1¼ in. to assemble the case. Pick up some 1-in. paneling nails to attach the back. For trim you'll need 3d finishing nails and ¾-in. and 1¼-in. brads.

9 | SHELF HARDWARE. Buy four 48-in.-long shelf standards, which you'll cut to fit inside the case. Standards come with a brass, white, or steel finish, and are usually sold with nails and shelf support clips.

10 | WOOD GLUE. Yellow wood glue is the best glue to use for this project.

11 | SANDPAPER. Get medium and fine sandpaper for your power sander and for hand-sanding.

12 | PRIMER, PAINT & STAIN. To paint the case, you'll need a quart of fast-drying primer and some latex paint. If you want to stain the top, get a half pint of stain.

DETAILS & DIMENSIONS

This cutaway view shows all the major parts of the bookcase. The case is really a big plywood box that's dressed up with a mitered 1x4 skirt and top rail and a few molding details.

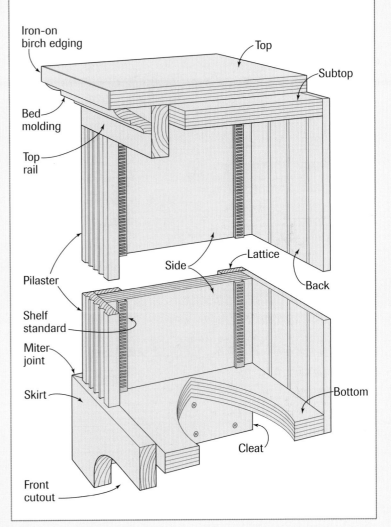

Assembling the Case

1 **CUT THE CASE PARTS.** Cut the back from a sheet of ¼-in. beaded paneling. Cut the sides, tops, bottom, and shelves from ¾-in. plywood. For the long cuts, guide your circular saw with a panel-cutting guide. Cut parts to length by guiding your saw against a large square. For smooth cuts, make sure to use a finish-cutting blade in your saw.

2 **ASSEMBLE THE CASE.** Use glue and 2-in. drywall screws to join the sides to the bottom and subtop. For easier assembly, try these tips: Attach a plywood cleat at the bottom of each side to support the bottom (see drawing on p. 113). Use bar clamps to keep case parts held together until you drive your screws. Before attaching the back, hold the case assembly square with a temporary diagonal brace. Wipe off glue squeeze-out with a damp cloth as you go.

3 **INSTALL THE SKIRT & TOP RAIL.** These 1x4 boards wrap around the front and sides of the case, with miter joints at the corners. Cut the miters in a miter box, and attach the skirt and top rail boards with glue and 4d finishing nails. Set these and other nails just below the surface using a nail set and hammer.

4 **MAKE THE SKIRT CUTOUT.** Trace against a small can to draw the curved corners of the cutout, then use your jigsaw to make the cut. To stay straight, tack a wood straightedge across the case to guide the edge of your saw's baseplate.

Remember to think "upside-down and backwards" when cutting bed molding and other cornice molding on your miter saw. The horizontal base of the miter saw represents the ceiling. The vertical fence of the saw represents the wall surface. To check your thinking and your mitering technique, cut and assemble a test corner against a square, as shown in the photo above.

Adding Details

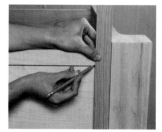

5 **INSTALL THE LATTICE TRIM.** Cut this thin molding in a miter box and attach it with glue and ¾-in. brads. Do the stiles (vertical pieces) first; then mark and cut the horizontal rails to fit between the stiles. The stretcher, made by nailing two boards together, takes the spring out of the side for nailing and ensures that the lattice is flush to the front edge.

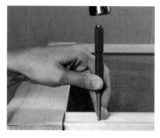

6 **INSTALL THE PILASTERS.** These two pieces fit between the skirt and top-rail boards, as shown in the drawing on p. 113. Cut them to fit using your miter box, then install with glue and 3d finishing nails. Check your alignment: The outside edge of the pilaster should be flush with the lattice molding on the side of the case.

7 **INSTALL THE TOP.** First, measure the top of the case, including the top rails. Next, cut your top piece 1½ in. wider and 3 in. longer than these measurements. Finish the front and end edges of the top with iron-on wood veneer tape. Then attach the top to the subtop with the case upside-down. Drive 1¼-in. screws through the subtop and into the top.

8 **INSTALL THE BED MOLDING.** This is the same molding we used on the bathroom cabinet (p. 32), and it's installed the same way, too. You can keep the case upside-down for this step. Use your miter saw to cut the miter joints where the molding meets at the corners. Attach the molding with glue and brads. You'll probably need 1¼-in. and ¾-in. brads, as shown in the photo. To avoid damaging the trim with hammer blows, use your nail set to finish driving each brad.

5 6

7 8

▶ DO IT RIGHT

A simple cutting jig will make it easier to cut shelf standards to length so they'll fit inside your case. Make sure to cut each standard from the same end, so the slots will align when your standards are installed.

✳ WHAT'S DIFFERENT?

Regular wood filler (aka putty) is great beneath a painted finish. But if you plan to stain bare wood, it's better to fill holes using a matching color wax filler stick after stain and varnish have been applied.

Finishing Touches

9   **MAKE THE SHELVES.** This case will hold three or four shelves comfortably. Cut each shelf from ¾-in. plywood, then glue and nail stop molding to the front edge for strength and appearance. Make sure to size your shelves to fit inside the case, taking the ¼-in. thickness of the shelf standards into account. Wipe off glue squeeze-out and sand each shelf thoroughly.

10   **SAND, PRIME & TAPE.** Use a random-orbit sander or a powered pad sander to smooth the flat areas. Sand corners, contours, and tight spots by hand. Remove dust with a vacuum, then wipe the piece down with a damp rag. If you plan to stain the top and bed molding (as we did here), mask off the bed molding with painter's masking tape. Apply primer with a 2½-in. brush. When the primer is dry to the touch, fill nail holes and cracks with putty (see WHAT'S DIFFERENT? at left).

11   **APPLY THE FINAL COATS.** Smooth any rough areas with 150-grit sandpaper, then apply two coats of paint to the case and shelves. When the paint has dried, mask off the top rail just below the bed molding and apply stain and varnish to the bed molding and the top.

12   **INSTALL STANDARDS, SHELVES & BOOKS.** Cut the standards equally and at least ⅛ in. shorter than the inside height of the case (see DO IT RIGHT at left). Fasten the standards to the sides using a spacer to hold them ¾ in. in from the back and front edges of case sides. Install your shelf supports and your shelves, then treat your favorite books to a new home. Rest up; your friends are going to want a bookcase just like this one.

9 10

11 12

Once built, your bookcase can get a single finish or several. The case shown here is finished with white semigloss enamel on the interior and medium-blue eggshell on the exterior. The crown molding and top have an "Early American" stain, topped with clear polyurethane varnish.

A good bookcase design leaves room for dimensional diversity: Make it tall and narrow or short and broad.

Become a cabinetmaker. It's not that difficult if you know how to construct a plywood case and then trim it out with a combination of stock moldings and solid wood. The nice thing about building your own bookcase is that you can get the dimensions, details, and finish just the way you want them; and you'll save plenty of money by doing the job yourself.

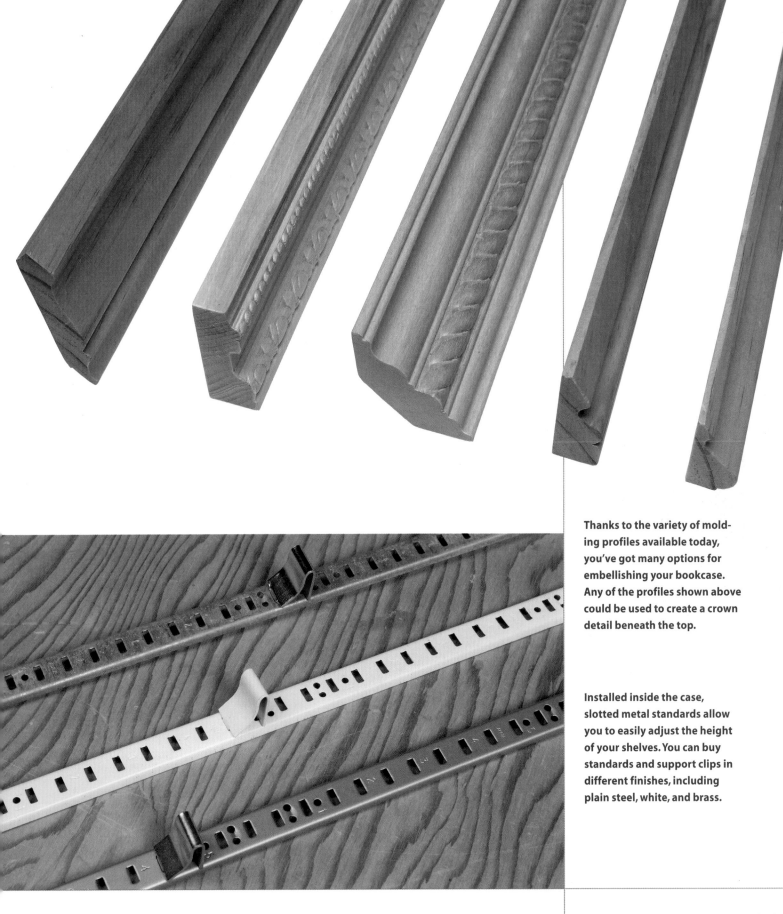

Thanks to the variety of molding profiles available today, you've got many options for embellishing your bookcase. Any of the profiles shown above could be used to create a crown detail beneath the top.

Installed inside the case, slotted metal standards allow you to easily adjust the height of your shelves. You can buy standards and support clips in different finishes, including plain steel, white, and brass.

For more great weekend project ideas look for these and other
TAUNTON PRESS BOOKS wherever books are sold.

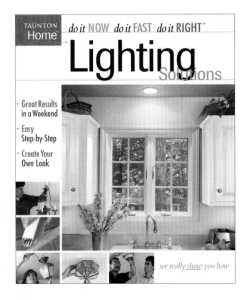

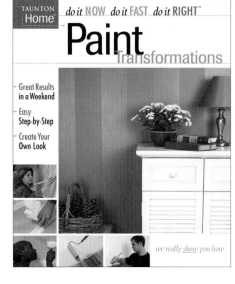

Lighting Solutions
1-56158-669-2
Product #070753
$14.95

Trim Transformations
1-56158-671-4
Product #070752
$14.95

Paint Transformations
1-56158-670-6
Product #070751
$14.95

For more information visit our Web site at www.doitnowfastright.com